Victor Canning

COMEDIES AND WHIMSIES

SHORT STORIES

PUBLISHED BY LULU.COM

This collection edited and with an introduction
by John Higgins

Shaftesbury, September 2015

Printed by permission of the Curtis Brown Group Ltd,
London, on behalf of the estate of Victor Canning.

ISBN: 978-1-326-43627-8

Contents

PREFACE

Victor Canning (1911- 1986) was a highly versatile and prolific writer, producing well over a hundred stories and novellas alongside his fifty-eight novels, two dozen television scripts, four radio plays, three stage plays and one travel book. Within the short stories he was also versatile, mixing crime and suspense with comedy. While it has to be admitted that some of the crime and thriller short stories are formulaic and hastily written, the stories in which he indulged his sense of comedy and whimsy tend to be much better. He creates real people who follow their instincts, rather than having them act in accordance with a contrived plot. He often puts them into backgrounds he knows rather than drawing exotic imaginary locations around them.

He used Wales as a setting in a part of only one of his novels, *The Hidden Face*, but he grew up and lived in the south west of England, did part of his military service in mid-Wales, and must have known many Welsh people. In the two stories he set in Wales he conveys the Welsh speech patterns effectively. "The Aberdyll Onion", published in *John Bull* in May 1959, is a first-person narrative in which the motivation for an apparent crime turns out to be very different from initial appearances. "The White Spell", also set in Wales, was published in *Lilliput* in May 1956 and describes the competition between three brothers for the hand of Helen, a beautiful local girl whom they have seen bathing in a mountain stream naked as only a husband should see her. She promises herself to the brother who wins the next sheepdog trials, and the plot concerns various tricks to bend the result. The story was illustrated in the magazine with a pretty line drawing of Helen bathing (which I have included) and this was enough to have the item in the British Library put on a restricted list for issue to adults only. Both Aberdyll and Llanidor, by the way, are fictitious places.

The story "Fighting Cockerel" came out in *Argosy* in November 1951 and is Canning's only use of Belfast as a setting. Once again he captures speech patterns well and tells a story of neighbourhood quarrels tinged with sectarianism and with an unpredictable ending.

Several of his stories were love stories. In "Arabella's Last Petticoat", published in various US newspapers in August 1958, the wooing is set in the context of nineteenth-century sailing ships trading between Britain and the Caribbean. In "Copy Coupon", published in the *Evening News* in December 1961, the setting is a London office and the characters are an unglamorous secretary and her unsuccessful boss. Also with a London setting is Canning's one and only ghost story, "Through the Wall", first published in the *Evening News* in October 1961. There are echoes in these two stories of Canning's early *Mr Finchley* books.

From the same period comes "Flight of Fancy", printed in the *Evening News* in November 1961 and reprinted in *Ellery Queen's Mystery Magazine* eight years later as "The Boy who Told Fibs". Modern society would not approve of the parent who plans to beat his child to teach him not to tell lies, but such attitudes were common enough then, and the parent in this case does at least change his mind.

Canning often introduced elderly eccentrics into his work, people like The General in *The Great Affair* and The Laird in *The Flight of the Grey Goose*. In two of his short stories such old codgers were given centre stage. In "Sanctuary for the General", which appeared in *Argosy* in August 1962, we meet Major-General Henry Braithwaite who takes extreme measures to block the building of a road across his land which would disturb a wildlife sanctuary. In "Vintage Vendetta", published in *Argosy* in the following month, we meet two elderly vintage car fanatics and watch them being manipulated by a pair of young lovers.

An early story, "The Ballerina and the Pigs" published in *John Bull* in November 1956, mixes exotic characters from an iron-curtain republic with homely agricultural themes, cider and pig-farming. Canning had already written one very good thriller, *A Forest of Eyes* (1950), set in Yugoslavia, and would go on to write another on the theme of a defecting ballerina being kidnapped and taken back to a communist regime, *The Limbo Line* (1963). Here the same topic is treated in a light-opera fashion with comically inept commissars and bucolic villagers thwarting them. I am reminded of Peter Ustinov's *Romanoff and Juliet*, which first appeared as a play in 1956 and on film five years later.

Canning used the theme of blindness very well in two of his crime stories. He also used colour-blindness as a plot device in two comic stories. In "Star Stuff", published in *Ellery Queen's Mystery Magazine* in March 1962, a director's colour-blindness frustrates the schemes of an ambitious actress. Canning worked extensively in film and television, so he had first-hand knowledge of that milieu, which is also evident in the next story, "She Knew what she Wanted", which appeared in *Woman's Own* in February, 1965. In "Death Wore Green", published in various US newspaper supplements in March 1957, we return to the theme of colour-blindness which nearly leads to the death of seaman Joe Barker. But all ends well, which is the way it should be in comedy.

Canning was not conventionally religious, but he wrote one short story that will be familiar to churchgoers, "Trouble in the City", which draws on the events of Palm Sunday. This appeared in *Argosy* in May 1962.

The next story, "The Lion Tamer", is one of the very first that Canning wrote. It was published in the *Evening Standard* in 1935 and presents a small slice of country life through the eyes of a ten-year-old boy, with a final ironic glimpse of the adult reality when the heroic strong-man is shown up as a hen-pecked husband. This is followed by two late stories. "A Friend of the Family", published in *Woman's Own* in 1974, blends a love story with Canning's newly reawakened passion for fishing. "The Daffodil Day", which appeared in *Woman's Own* in April 1981, is an account of a day excursion and a strange young man who hitches a ride and then seems able to solve everybody's problems. The theme is almost exactly that of Canning's last book, *Table Number Seven*, so that this story looks like a preliminary sketch for that book.

The collection ends with a story that has not been previously published as far as I know. "Through the Eyes of Love" is a rather sentimental account of an elderly confidence trickster yielding to his conscience. The setting is Plymouth, Canning's own birthplace. The typescript was found in the files of Curtis Brown, Canning's agent and probably dates from 1982.

In the 1940s and '50s many newspapers published fiction, at least one item a day in the *Evening Standard* for instance. Canning himself never rated his stories highly; for him they were just items he dashed off to earn a few pounds (typically £3 or £4 in the 1930s,

£25 in the 1950s) and keep commuters distracted for a few minutes of their journey. The short story market dried up as the popularity of television grew, and Canning wrote very few stories after 1965. But most of what he wrote has retained its appeal and can still entertain us just as well today.

John Higgins, Shaftesbury, September 2015

A website covering the life and works of Victor Canning is maintained at:

http://www.victorcanning.com

Tragedy and comedy sometimes share the same bed. Both are restless sleepers.

(Victor Canning, *The Doomsday Carrier*, p. 198)

THE ABERDYLL ONION

Although it was only eleven o'clock in the morning, Sir John gave me a glass of whisky and a cigar as thick as a broom handle, and sat me down in a great leather armchair.

"Hughes," he said to me, "how long have you lived in Aberdyll?"

"Seventy years," I said. He knew it as well as I did, but Sir John was a great one for telling and asking people things. Little, fat chap he was, with a bald head and a ginger moustache, and a temper to go with it. I wish I had all the money he's made out of Aberdyll Onion Soup, Aberdyll Welsh Broth, Aberdyll Asparagus Tips, and so on, and all in tins.

"And not a thing goes on here but that you don't know all or something about it, eh?"

I nodded. "More or less, Sir John."

"And that's why I asked you to come up here, Hughes. Got a little job for you. Fifty pounds if you bring it off. A little detective work."

"Wouldn't that be more in the line of Jones the Police?" I asked.

"P.C. Jones? No. Good fellow, but he could be in it. Never know what a man will do when it comes to horticultural pride. He's after the Aberdyll Cup too, you know."

"Ah," I said. "About the onion is it, then?"

"It is, Hughes. Some scoundrel has stolen Williams's onion. Two years he's won my cup, and from what I could see was likely to win it again this year. That would give him the cup for good and five hundred pounds. Wonderful publicity it would be for our soups."

Sir John ran on a bit, telling me about the Aberdyll Onion Cup as though I knew nothing about it. Every year there was a great competition for this cup at the Aberdyll Show. But more than that, Sir John used it for publicity for his tinned soups.

The Aberdyll Onion was something special. In all the papers each year. Entries limited to amateur growers in Aberdyll. Always a good deal of feeling about it in Aberdyll. Sometimes you'd get so that you didn't want to hear another word about onions … the right soil and fertilizers, and so on. Well — some of the chaps used to sit up at nights with their onions, talking to them, maybe … egging them on.

"Keep your ear to the ground, make some inquiries, Hughes," Sir John was saying now, "Let me know what scoundrel took Williams's onion. I'll make him regret it."

And he would, too, with that old temper and a J.P., too. So I promised to do what I could and went off to see Williams the Onion — that's what they call him, seeing he'd won the cup twice and had looked like winning it outright.

Dark, quiet young chap he was, strong chapel man, a porter on the railway, and a broken-hearted man. That onion might have been his favourite child.

"I'm telling you, man," he said, "it was in the garden at half past seven. I was working there. And then I come in for a bite of supper" — he's a bachelor and looks after himself in a bit of a cottage behind the station — "and go out again at half past eight just to see it's all right and maybe cover it from the heavy dew, and it's gone. A real shock. Day before yesterday it was. Big as a football almost. There's a lovely colour it was, too."

"Who would you say had the nearest chance of beating you?" I asked him.

"Let's see now. Jones the Police might. Then there's Morgan the Waterworks. And Evans the Pub. Nobody else would have a chance. My own seed, you know. Special. Nothing left now but a big hole dug clean in the ground, man. No doubt whatever, whoever did it took all that soil so they could analyse it and find out my secret feeding. I just can't go through the garden now, Hughes, *bach …*"

"No footprints in the soil?"

"Nothing. They could stand on the concrete path and dig it up."

Well, I went along first of all to Jones the Police's place. He was out on his beat, but Mrs Jones, a sharp little woman with four children, opened the door to me and out with it came a delicious smell of stew, rich and oniony. But as I sniffed at it Mrs. Jones said to me, a little quick like: "Our own onions, Mr. Hughes, and between half past seven and half past eight the night before last Jones was watching the telly with me and the kids. And now, if you'll pardon me, I'll have to go and take that stew off before it burns."

With Morgan up at the waterworks it was different. He invited me in and gave me a glass of beer and said: "Hughes, *bach*, I'm a timid man. All my life I've lacked courage. Big dreams have been my share, but only little actions. That's why I read so much. I live in the imagination, man. I lack the courage to live in the real world."

He went on: "We Morgans are poets. Dreamers not doers. Otherwise I might have stolen Williams's onion. Think of it, man — a soft summer night, full of the smell of the warm earth, shadows, a solitary light from a cottage window and me, spade in hand, stealing like cut-throat through the gloom ... There's a picture, look you." He put his hands in front of him and said: "Put the handcuffs on me, lead me away to prison and I'll write the Ballad of Aberdyll Jail."

Well, poet he might be, but a little drunk always was, and he didn't have to tell me that between half past seven and half past eight on the night he'd been down at the Aberdyll Arms.

And that's where I went to see Evans the Pub. I went in the back way, which is along a dark little passage, and as I passed through the door someone coming out bumped into me. It was young Phillips the Rolls, that is Sir John's chauffeur — a good-looking, well set up young fellow with fair hair.

I said: "If you're going up to the Hall to drive Sir John out somewhere, Phillips, you'd better wipe the lipstick off your face." Slap in middle of his right cheek it was, and he looked proper foolish.

Half-way down the passage, Nancy Evans was tidying her hair in a wall mirror. Now you couldn't miss Nancy, dark, all curves and as good-natured as a spaniel. I pinched her bottom and went into the bar and she went round behind the counter and pulled me my usual glass of half-and-half. As she handed it to me she said: "That's thirty shillings you've got on the slate, Mr. Hughes."

"I'm expecting a legacy at the end of the week," I said. "Where's your da?"

"In Cardiff where he has been these last three days — so if you're snooping around about the old onion you can forget it. My da wouldn't do such a thing."

"Your da," I said, "would give you a tanning if he caught you kissing young Phillips. And so would Williams the Onion. I thought you two were promised?"

"We've been walking out for three years. It's a long promise. And young Phillips is a mannerly chap."

"If Williams won the cup this year, he'd have five hundred pounds. More than enough to set up a house," I said. "If someone didn't want you and him to marry, look you, it's tempted to pinch the old onion they might be to give themselves more time to get you to change your mind."

"If pigs had wings, they'd fly."

"And where were you between half past seven and half past eight night before last?"

"Looking for gold at the foot of the rainbow, Mr. Hughes." She was a saucy piece but I liked her.

"And where was young Phillips?"

"How should I know?"

"Then I must have been dreaming," I said, "because on my way here that night I could have sworn I seen him and you sitting on the railway embankment, not far from Williams's cottage. The foot of that rainbow must have been mighty narrow for you were both squeezed very tight to get under it."

"At your age," said Nancy, "you want glasses."

"I see well enough. Still, though the onion's been stolen, no harm's done."

"What's that?" she asked.

"Williams is no fool. He means to get that cup and the money. I wouldn't tell you this if you weren't practically his fiancée, but he's got another little patch of ground up behind the rectory. He's been growing another prize onion there in secret."

I finished my beer and went out and when I was safely away I couldn't help chuckling at the memory of Nancy's face. I may be old, but there's nothing you can teach me about love.

It was as clear as day that Nancy didn't want to marry Williams any more, and that between her and young Phillips they had done away with the onion. All I had to do was to watch in the little bit of ground behind the rectory that warm summer night and I was sure that either Nancy or Phillips would appear to steal the other onion.

4

So, just before dark I got up to the little bit of ground by the rectory and made myself comfortable between a couple of gooseberry bushes.

I waited there for about two hours and then things began to happen. There was a noise at the far end of the ground, and then another at my end, and then right across the way from me I heard somebody stumble against a wheelbarrow.

I stood up and switched on a torch and swung it round in a circle. First of all I saw young Nancy and Phillips, blinking in the light like a couple of young owls. Then, swaying by the wheelbarrow was Morgan the Waterworks, and away on my left was Jones the Police.

I gave a little laugh and shook my head. Pretty sheepish they all looked.

"Welcome friends," I said. "Nancy's been talking in the pub, is it? And you've all come to steal the onion."

P.C. Jones, who was in uniform, drew himself up and said with dignity, "I'm here to protect it. Same as you, *bach.*"

Morgan comes weaving across to me. his eyes shining, and said: "Morgan becomes a doer. Found my courage at last, man. I've come for that onion."

"So have Nancy and I," said young Phillips, with his arms round Nancy. "And we would have taken the first if we'd thought of it. We love each other and she don't want to go through with it with Williams. Can't see any girl wanting to be known as Mrs. Williams the Onion for the rest of her life."

"That's right," said Nancy. "Mrs. Phillips the Rolls for me. I love him."

I looked around at them all and then I said: "You'd better all go home and I'll forget about this. Williams hasn't got a second onion up here."

You should have seen their faces. Anyway, after a bit of argument they left. But I sat there a while, thinking like. Then I went to see Williams.

"Williams," I said, "there's practising a deceit you've been."

"Go away, Hughes, *bach,*" he said. "I am on the horns of a dilemma."

"True," I said. "Proper stuck, too, you are." I told him what I had done, and I finished: "But none of the people that come up to the

5

rectory had so much as a spade in their hands. They were going to pull up the onion. But your own was dug up. The work of a true onion lover who couldn't bear to damage so much as a hair of a root."

I walked to a little recess in the corner of the kitchen and pulled the curtain back. There, planted neat and beautiful in the centre of a wooden tub, was the onion. Man, it was a size.

"Why did you do it?" I asked.

He shook his head. "It's this dilemma," he said. "If I'd have won the prize this year I'd have got five hundred pounds, and then I would have had to marry Nancy. We're promised."

"And you don't want to marry her?"

"No, man, I don't. She's a nice enough girl. But my heart is with that old onion and everything that grows. What I want is to take that five hundred and start a nursery garden business with it. That would mean a lot of hard work and no time until much later for marriage. But I'm a man of honour —"

I said: "Williams, *bach,* if you'd had eyes for anything but your onion you'd have saved yourself a lot of trouble. Put it back and win the prize. You don't have to break your word to Nancy. She wants to marry Phillips the Rolls. She don't want to be Mrs. Williams the Onion."

"She don't?"

"Put it back and I'll tell Sir John some story that'll cover it for you and also do me no harm so far as my fifty pounds is concerned."

You should have seen the way he went over and lifted that tub so lovingly. Once a man like Williams falls in love with a vegetable, his eyes are closed to all women.

THE
WHITE SPELL

*"You've seen me as only
a husband should," said Helen. "Now one
of you must marry me."*

THE WHITE SPELL

Harry's Bar is in Venice and the two of us were drinking martinis. He said he was an Australian sheep farmer on his way to England, and his voice had a lot of Welsh in it. And, of course, there was the dog. It had strayed in out of the heat and we were feeding it occasional potato crisps.

My friend had sad, romantic eyes, a humorous mouth and a wallet that bulged inside his silk jacket. He gave the dog a pat and said, "Somewhere in him I swear there's a touch of Welsh sheep dog. In fact, if I shut my eyes and squint and pretend that he's black and white instead of brown, he could be the dead spit of Jason."

"And who was Jason?" I asked.

"A dog," he said. "The best. I'll tell you about him. As quick as a mountain stream, as quiet as night, a clever as the devil, and what he didn't know about sheep you could have written on an ear of corn …"

High poetry and a more pronounced Welsh accent came into his voice as he got going. In the little Welsh hill town of Llanidor, it seemed, there were three brothers; John Evans, twenty-four and the eldest; Idris Evans, twenty-three; and then Morgan Evans, the youngest, twenty-two, and they were the sons of a well-to-do sheep farmer. Each brother had a sheep dog, but Jason belonged to John and the dogs of the other brothers couldn't compare with it. Each year when the town held its local show it was John with Jason who won the sheep dog trials.

Now the rivalry of the brothers over their dogs was innocent enough. Less innocent, however, was their rivalry over a woman.

"It's in love they all were," said my friend. "Hopelessly, fightingly in love with a woman. Her name was Helen and more beautiful than that other who put the cat among the pigeons at Troy or wherever it was."

He went on for some time, about Helen, but finally came round to the point. The Evans brothers would all inherit well from their father who owned several farms and Helen, while she didn't favour one more than the other, let it be seen that it was between one of them and the son of Williams, the pub. The pub, in fact, was a fine hotel — the Llanidor Arms and worth having.

Then one day young Williams was put right out of the running. The three Evans brothers had been up in the hills going over their sheep for fly- and foot-rot and, on their way home, feeling hot and tired they stripped off by the side of a stream and bathed. After their swim they lay down naked in the grass in the sun and went to sleep.

Well, after a time they were awakened by the sound of someone singing. It was a woman's voice and, since they were naked, the young men sat up very quietly and cautiously and looked round.

"The sight that met their eyes," said my friend, "was idyllic, classical, right out of *Daphnis and Chloë* and there wasn't a man in Llanidor, or anywhere else for that matter, who wouldn't have given fifty pounds for the privilege which was theirs.

"In the middle of the pool, and the drought of summer had made it run shallow, was Helen. She was standing there as God made her, and as she sang to herself she was lifting the cool water in her hands and pouring it over the fairest body in the Principality of Wales and far beyond. The Evans brothers just sat there and watched the flash of water like quicksilver on her fair skin and the golden stream of her hair over her shoulders."

And then Helen had seen them. But she was a girl of great self-control. She crouched down until the water came to her shoulders and she said firmly, "John Evans, Idris Evans, and you, too, is it, Morgan Evans — I'll thank you all to shut your eyes until I'm out of this pool."

They did as they were told. When she had disappeared they put on their own clothes like men in a dream. In a few moments she came round to them, dressed now, and carrying herself like a queen.

"You've seen me mother naked," said Helen, who was not a girl to mince her words and could cast a column of figures more accurately and quickly than any bank clerk. "That's a thing should rest between man and wife. If I married anyone else in the valley now, as might be Williams the pub, you'd go round the rest of your lives with a knowing twitch to your lips and a snigger in your hearts. It's only human. Fortunately, I like you all well enough and now one of you must marry me."

"I'll brain them both if they so much as breathe it once we're married," said John, turning on the other two.

"I'll go to Cardiff for the ring tomorrow," said Idris squaring up to John.

9

"You stood in the water like a nymph," said Morgan dreamily. "Even the birds forgot to sing when they saw you. We'll go straight to the minister now and arrange the banns."

In another moment they would all have been at one another. But Helen had her own method for choosing which one it should be.

"I like you all," she said. "Not a pin between you. And I'll have no fighting over the matter. I'll marry the one of you who wins the sheep dog trials."

John Evans was content enough with this. He'd won the trials for the last three years. But the other two were in their different ways, determined to stop him from winning the trial this year. Idris was originally for poisoning Jason, but the dog would only take food from John and for every minute of the next two weeks John kept Jason with him night and day. Idris in the end got a new dog for which he paid fifty pounds and spent the time remaining to him working it. Morgan, who was no poisoner of dogs and too fond of his own little bitch, Meg, to change her, went to Widow Pandy who was by way of being a part-time witch and asked her help.

"Is it a spell that looks natural or sudden death for Jason you want?" she asked. "The first is more expensive."

"A natural spell," said Morgan.

"A hundred pounds, then," said Widow Pandy. "It's an amount I need badly. I will give you a white spell."

"Any sum, whatever," said Morgan dreamily. "Helen is beyond price."

"To be paid the day after your marriage and not a thing will you have to do, Morgan Evans, but work your dog Meg in the trials as always."

Well, the great day came, blistering hot and a fine crowd to watch the sheep dog finals.

The way the trial was worked was this; a flock of sheep was penned at the top of a long furze-spangled slope of hill. A handler let five of them out of the pen and from the bottom of the hill the shepherd sent away his dog to collect them and bring them down. On the way down they had to be passed through two hurdle gates, and then one sheep had to be shed — that is, left behind — and the four remaining brought on and penned in a small hurdle corral at the bottom of the hill.

Including the Evans brothers there were six shepherds in the final, but everyone knew it was going to be between the brothers. The three outsiders turned in good times. Then Morgan's turn came and when the sheep were loosed he sent away Meg. She shed one and had the other four penned in eight minutes fourteen seconds. Good time, but not championship stuff.

Then came Idris's turn with his new dog. He shed the first sheep in fine time but after that the whole thing went to pieces. One of the sheep was plain stubborn and awkward. So he went roaring up to the judges and shouted that the awkward sheep must have been blind.

"Blind, man!" laughed John Evans. "Look you, it's your dog that's blind."

Then came John's turn. John Evans — and you should have seen the dark scowl on his face — did worse than Idris. He never even got to shedding the first sheep, let alone penning four at the bottom of the hill. Jason, the dog, did all that a dog could do; but a couple of those sheep wandered and trotted around like drunken sailors. Oh, there was hell to pay! John finally gave up and went storming up to the judges. Two of his sheep were blind, he swore. But the judges wouldn't have it. They examined the sheep and found nothing wrong with them — and so they named Morgan the winner. Naturally, there was a bit of a fight after that, you know, between the brothers. But in the end Morgan wedded his Helen. And he paid the hundred pounds to Widow Pandy, who needed it because her son wanted to emigrate to Australia and become a sheep farmer. Which he did. And fine and prosperous he became."

He pulled out his bulging wallet and called for two more martinis.

"And you," said I, seeing through him easily, "are Widow Pandy's son? How did the spell, work then?"

"Widow Pandy's son? Ah, yes — he worked the spell for her. He was handling the sheep at the top of the hill. When he let Idris's lot out he smacked a good dab of his mother's butter in the eye of one beast. And he did the same for two of John's beasts. This blinded them in one eye for about five minutes, but by the time the judges got to them the butter had run and looked like sweat in the fleece around their eyes and they could see well enough. But I'm not Widow Pandy's son. He has the next place to me in Australia. I'm

Morgan Evans, look you. After two years with Helen I couldn't stand her any longer and I left her and emigrated."

FIGHTING COCKEREL

I mind the day I first went as a lodger in Barney Doran's house. I wasn't more than a stripling, though I was big for my age and, in those days, I felt I had the world by the tail and was twisting it hard. Barney looks at me and he says, "It's a dirty, unwholesome job ye've got workin' on a newspaper, but I'll take ye in — for your morals will not have been corrupted yet. What'll ye go stripped? About a hundred and thirty pounds, devil a bit more or I'm no judge?"

I might have been a bit puzzled if the lads at the paper had not told me about the old man. In a life which had been full of its fair share of devilry, excitement and decent hard work — though Barney never professed any overdue liking for this last — the old man had been a boxer. And a good one, too, though he was now past it by about twenty years.

"You're right there," I says, "a hundred and twenty-eight."

"Sure, and wasn't I the same at your age."

He looks at me hard and for the moment there was no twinkle at the back of his hard blue eyes. "Do ye think we was fair beat at the Boyne?"

Barney was no Orangeman, and that again was one of the reasons they'd sent me along to him. "You needn't worry over the colours I'll wear on the Twelfth of July," I says, and with that the interviewing was done and Barney set me down with a glass on a chair outside the window and we sat and talked and he told me a lot about himself. A rare, fine talker he was, with just enough imagination to keep a story going without giving anyone cause to name him a liar. Then, just as we were thinking of going in, he says,

"It's an important question I'll ask ye now, so you'll not be saying Barney Doran had ye here under false pretences. Are ye a good sleeper?"

"I never had any trouble," I says.

"Then ye're a lucky man," says Barney, "and I'm hopin' your luck keeps runnin'. I sleep bad meself. Not a decent night's sleep I've known in a long time."

"And why would that be?" I asks him.

"Come with me and I'll show ye the cause av it all," he says, and with that he rises and we go to the bottom of the garden. On the other side of the fence was a strip of land used as a fowl-yard which belonged to Barney's neighbour, Michael Taafe. In the yard were a few white hens and, sitting on top of a box, as fine a cockerel as ever I'd seen.

"There he is," says Barney. "Yon brawlin' braggart murders me sleep ivery mornin'."

Just then the bird begins to crow. It was the evening performance and never did I hear such a noise. The creature seemed fair demented with pride and vigour. It threw back its head and crowed and crowed until it was a wonder it didn't break a blood vessel. Man, it was so fantastic I had to laugh. Sure, and at the same time I couldn't help admiring the bird. It was one of the most beautiful I'd ever seen, with a tawny mantle that fell from its shoulders in a rich, warm gold; its tail feathers had the arch and sweep of an emperor's plumes, green and blue and afire with sheen, and the red of its wattles and the yellow of its legs were as bright as new paint.

"It's a useless devil," says Barney. "You'll hear him at five ivery mornin', tellin' the world what a fine fellow he is. Would ye credit now that such a small body could give out that amount av noise, and all for the admiration of its own useless self? One mornin' I'll take me gun to it, and that'll be the end!"

As Barney was saying this, there comes down to the bottom of the next garden his neighbour, Michael Taafe. Taafe was as old as Barney, but taller, wirier and with not enough meat on his bones to keep his clothes company.

"If iver ye harm that bird, Barney Doran," he says, "I'll have the law on ye."

"Will ye then?" answers Barney. "Maybe ye think ither people is as scared of the law as ye've reason to be?"

They passed a few compliments to one another, and if it hadn't been for Taafe's wife calling to him to come in for supper I'd not have been surprised to see them over the fence at one another.

Later, I learned that Barney and Taafe had been on similar terms for many years. Apart from their political persuasions which, of course, made the whole thing reasonable and entirely natural —

Barney being a Nationalist and Taafe an Orangeman — there was also the matter of a small piece of land which Barney owned that lay over the other side of a small stream which bordered Taafe's fowl-yard. Taafe wanted to buy the land and Barney had no intention of selling it at any price, though devil a use did he put the land to himself.

"You should make a complaint to the police," I says one day after I'd been there for some time, for I could see that with an old man like Barney the loss of his sleep was doing him no good.

"I'll make no complaint," says Barney. "But one mornin' that bird will go too far and I'll take me gun to it."

He was always saying he would shoot the bird, but I knew he never would. He was at heart a good-natured man, not the kind to blow an innocent bird into eternity. But each morning, when the cockerel would begin his blathering, Barney would turn in his bed in the room next to mine and there would be a muttering, and then the window would go up with a bang and Barney would lean out in his nightshirt and curse it with a fluency which was an education in itself to a young man like myself just entering the newspaper trade.

Then, after I'd been there about three months, the whole thing came to a head. One morning in July the bird woke me with its crowing and I heard the bang of Barney's window.

"Hush your bawlin', ye painted heathen!" he shouts. "Do ye want me to come and silence ye?"

But the bird only answers him with a clamour fit to wake the dead.

"Ye roarin' braggart —" shouts Barney, "— have ye no respect or decency in your carcase?"

The bird let fly another screech that set the echoes ringing between the houses and I heard Barney shout some more. Then his window went down with a bang the way it was a wonder the glass stood up to it. After a bit I thought I heard Barney downstairs. I lay listening, wondering what the old man was up to. Suddenly there was an awful rattle of echoes against the house as someone fired a shotgun.

Even as I jumped out of bed I said to myself, "Barney, you've done the wrong thing." When I looked out of the window there was Barney at the bottom of the garden, just climbing over the fence into the fowl-yard, and in his hand he carried a smoking shot gun. I pulled on some clothes and ran down. I got into the fowl-yard just as Michael Taafe came tearing through, angry and half-asleep, with his nightshirt tucked into his trousers and his braces trailing behind him like a forked tail.

Barney was standing in the yard holding the shotgun in the crook of his arm, and he had the cockerel held against his breast with his free hand. The bird seemed half-dead, with its eyes lidding over, and the blood was coming from a bad wound in its neck.

"Ye murderin' villain!" screams Michael Taafe. "You shot me bird! I'll have the law on ye for this! You dirty assassin — I've a mind to teach you some decent behaviour meself!"

"Hold your noise, you stupid ould woman," says Barney, " 'Twas you was the instigator av the whole trouble. Do ye want to provoke me?"

Taafe's braces flopped about in the dust as he danced up and down.

"You needn't think you'll come out av this so aisily … Give me the bird!"

"Ye'll not get the bird," says Barney. "If any bird deserved to be shot this one did. If ye're takin' the law av me," says Barney, "ye'll no doubt get your damages. Meantime I'm keepin' the bird, and if you try and take him from me I'll wipe your eye for you and be obliged to wash me hands after …"

Although Barney was fairly calm against Taafe's rage, I'll not say he was being exactly conciliatory, and there was a fair gathering of neighbours around by now, some of them in their nightshirts and some in more decent modes of dress, but all taking a great personal interest in the affair. There were those who felt like Barney — the bird had been a plague to them. But there were others who were for Taafe, because as is natural a man must follow his political feelings regardless of the right or wrong of his cause.

When Barney offered to wipe Taafe's eye, Taafe — with no lack of spirit — says, "And I'd like to see the man who could now. It'll certainly not be you on this day."

And that did it, of course, for we all suddenly remembered what the day was. Sure, it was the Twelfth of July, and even without the bird it would have been fair reason for the larrikins that ensued.

Barney dropped the bird and the gun and went into Taafe like a mole tunnelling a potato patch, and when a neighbour — it was Con

McGra — tried to part them he got a swipe on the head from Taafe that knocked him into the chicken hut. Seeing that Barney had McGra with him, it was the proper duty of Big Pete Armstrong to join in to make things even for Taafe. And when Big Pete was in, Danny the Pump joins in for Barney. After a little while, what with one joining in and then another, and no chance of ever getting the odds evened up, it was each man for himself and an occasional woman hanging about the outskirts to bang you over the head with a bat of wood or a garden paling just to keep you in the tight in case you had a mind to up and sneak away before the thing was properly settled — which, in fairness to both sides, I must say was an idea that never once crossed the minds of any of us.

The only complaint I heard afterwards was that the rising dust from the bare earth made it hard to settle who was for or against you, so that there were quite a few that found themselves pitched into the small brook at the edge of the yard by good friends who would never have raised a hand against them if they could have seen properly.

I finished in the brook, but I had the satisfaction of sending one or two there first to establish its fitness for myself, and both Barney and Taafe came in with me. It was while we were getting our wind and thinking of coming out that Father Gorrian arrives and stops the fight. He said some hard words, and there was no arguing with him for his judgment was that on the civil side Barney was in the wrong, though on the religious side he was in the right since a man has a duty to fight for his religion. But that is as it may be. Barney and I went back to the house, and Barney took the bird and his gun with him.

Taafe went back to his house and that day started legal proceedings against Barney for the loss of the bird and also for assault and battery.

"I should av kept me temper, both wi' the bird and wi' Taafe," says Barney inside the house. "Not that I regret anything. No, 'twas as decent a fight, considerin' the day, as a man could ask for."

With that he starts to fuss over the bird. He spent a great deal of time for the next two days over the cockerel, and gradually he got him back to health. It was a miracle of patience how he did it, but done it was, and it seemed to me he wanted to do it as a sort of recompense, for it was not like Barney to shoot at a defenceless bird in that way.

17

Taafe, of course, brought a charge and the affair became the talk of the town. You see, it wasn't only a question of the bird. It was a question of one faction against another, and when Barney was brought up before the magistrates the place was crowded and Major Dundas had to threaten to clear the place unless people behaved themselves. He was a good man, the major, and although of the same political persuasion as Barney he indulged in no prejudice which any man, in the circumstances, could call unreasonable.

"Ye've heard all the evidence, Barney," he says, "and while I'm not taking into account the political differences involved, for this is no place for them, I'm a little surprised at you. If it had been anyone else but a good Irishman like yourself," and with that he gives a glance towards that part of the court which was packed with Michael Taafe's men, "I could have understood it. But ye're not the kind of man to take a shot at a sitting bird. Why on earth did ye not come and make a complaint in the proper way?"

"Well, your honour," says Barney, "he was disturbin' me sleep and I could stand it no longer. Your honour knows, 'tis a patient man I am, and for months I've stood the yammerin' av that orange-backed, crowin' Billy —"

"Just refer to it as the bird," says the Major with a pleased twist to his face. "There's some in this court would think your reference of 'crowin' Billy' had something to do with the good King William whose memory is evergreen in our loyal hearts."

"Sure, your honour," says Barney. "Well, I'd sworn I'd not be forced to law by this … creature. But that mornin' me temper took the upper hand of me. It's sleep that is a precious thing when ye've reached my age, your honour — as I'm prayin' ye'll live long enough to know for yourself one of these days."

"You shouldn't have shot him, Barney," says the Major. "Ye did wrong."

"I'm not denyin' it," says Barney. "Live and let live. But there it is, your honour. As for the fight afterwards, well — as Father Gorrian has said — there was provocation on both sides, and maybe a deal more on one than the ither —"

"Quite, quite," says the Major, and then after a bit more talk the upshot was that Barney was fined five pounds damages which he paid into the court there and then.

18

When he came out I was with him, and Michael Taafe comes up.

"Barney Doran," he says, "I'd like me bird back. I understand he's in your house and well recovered."

But Barney shakes his head. "Ye've had your five pounds, Taafe. I'm keepin' the bird," and then he added, sounding a bit embarrassed, "— and if ye don't think that's fair enough, I'll let ye buy that piece of land ye've wanted all along."

So Barney kept the cock and sold his land. He kept the bird in a little run he made in the garden and fetched it a couple of hens for company, but it never crowed again. The injury to its neck had finished its crowing, and all it could do was to give a few clucks now and again. Barney used to sit on a chair watching it. It was very strange how attached he was to the creature now.

Then one day he says, "Ye're wonderin' why I'm so fond av that bird? Ye can't understand it, can ye?"

"Well," says I, "it's just that I can't put the two things comfortably together — you, shooting the bird, and then being so affectionate towards it."

"Faith," says Barney, "seein' that it's real fond av ye I am, I'll tell ye now. But if iver ye breathe a word of it to anyone in this town, I'll wipe your eye for ye."

"I'll not risk that," I says. "What is it now?"

"Well," says Barney, "I was after the blood av that cockerel that mornin'. 'Tis that what counts. I meant murder. That's why I never denied it to the Major — for ye must know that it isn't doin' the deed that makes a man guilty, it's decidin' to do it.

"No. I went down to the empty braggart that mornin' to kill him, but when I got there the crowin' had stopped — and for good reason. There was a weasel in the yard, a long, slim devil of a beast come in after the young birds. There they was, all cooped up in a corner like frightened women folk, and our friend here was havin' a rare set-to with the weasel. Man, he showed me then he wasn't any empty braggart and me heart warmed to him. There he was, jumpin' and leapin', and them wicked spurs going right, left, right, left, as neat and clever as any boxer. But the weasel was no fool, either. He got on to the bird's neck and drew blood bad, but the cockerel threw him off and kept going for his eyes.

19

"That ould bird knew how to fight, and there was me standin' there that had had him marked for an empty, crowin' rascal for months. Man, the way that bird fought, he had a right to crow. In the end he had the weasel blinded and the beast ran round in circles trying to get out of the yard. That's when I fired. I didn't want the weasel to be away blinded, to die like a miserable sinner in a hole. I finished him wi' a shot and he fell into the brook yonder. Then you all came tearin' down on me …"

"But Barney," says I, "why did you not tell us?"

"What was there to tell ye? I meant to kill the bird. I would have done it but for that weasel, and then I would have had his blood on me hands. No, as one fighter to another, I was glad to pay the five pounds for him."

ARABELLA'S LAST PETTICOAT

My grandfather, who is eighty-two, said, "Once a year you dine with me at this club and each year your tie gets louder. Have some more port." He passed the decanter and went on, "And I don't suppose you'd come at all if you didn't think that one day I'll leave you some money, eh?"

"I come for your company, sir," I said, "not for your money."

"Then you're a damn fool, my boy." He smiled. "Any youngster your age should keep a weather eye open for the main chance. What are you? Thirty-odd?"

"Thirty-four."

"Got a wife lined up yet?"

"No, sir."

"Then you should have. Though I can see it's difficult to pick a woman these days. How can you tell what's in a sack until you open it up? Thirty-four, eh? My father — that's your great-grandfather — was that age when he married. Ever tell you the story of his marriage?"

"No, sir."

"Then you're lucky. Every other man in this club has heard it ad nauseam …" He began to prepare a cigar and not another word did he say until it was lit and drawing well.

"My father — your great-grandfather, Sir Thomas Ancaster, though he wasn't knighted then, of course — stood six feet two in his socks, had hair as dark as night and, at the age of thirty-four, he had the world in his hand like an oyster and he knew the knife wasn't going to slip as he opened it up. He was the master of the barkentine *Persephone* trading between Bristol and Port au Prince in Haiti. Rum, molasses, tobacco, and a few passengers.

"There was a fleet of six ships and they were owned by a James Sparkman, a rich man, a hard man, but fair. Sparkman had one daughter, Arabella Sparkman, about twenty-three at the time, proud, beautiful, fair-haired and with the temper of the devil. The first time she came aboard the *Persephone* — Tom Ancaster was taking her from Port au Prince to England — Tom fell in love with her. Within

21

twenty-four hours he'd asked her to marry him, pressed his suit a little too hard, had his face slapped and was told to 'keep his place'."

But Tom Ancaster, according to my grandfather, was a man who had very definite ideas about his place in life. He had no intention of always being a barkentine captain. He was a big man with big ideas.

Arabella spent a year in England and, whenever he had time, Tom Ancaster went to London and somehow managed to get to the same parties. But it did him no good. The fair Arabella was after bigger game.

"At the end of the year," said my grandfather, "she came down to Bristol to embark on the *Persephone* to return to her father in Port au Prince. She was more or less engaged now to some young sprig in London, but Tom didn't let that worry him. With a three week voyage ahead of them he set out to prove that he was the only man for her. And when he set out to sell himself, he could be irresistible — but not to Arabella. Don't think Tom didn't have his eye to the main chance. He did. Arabella was Sparkman's daughter. Sparkman was getting old, and Tom had no objection to picking up a shipping line as well as a wife. But also he was in love with her. Love, these days, is a light word, my boy. But in those days men used to get it like a fire in the belly. It didn't put a man like Tom off his food. Made him eat more. Wanted all the strength he could to fight for what he wanted."

When the *Persephone* was some weeks out, Tom Ancaster sprang a surprise for Arabella. It was her birthday and he gave a party for her in his cabin. He put on a splendid dinner, had three or four of the hands form an orchestra so that the few passengers could dance after the meal. Arabella turned up at the party wearing an enormous white crinoline and with her arms and shoulders bare.

"My boy, women in those days could carry all the canvas in the world, full-rigged and splendid. But they never left you guessing, like they do today, whether they were as Nature made them or some leaky craft held together by paint and hoping to catch the eye with false bows …"

He expanded on this point for a while and then got back to the story. Apparently just after the party had finished and the guests had retired, the *Persephone* was found to be on fire. How it happened no one ever knew for certain. Maybe one of the hands had been smoking in the forehold, or a lamp had been knocked over. Anyway, within an hour the *Persephone* was well ablaze and nothing could be done except abandon ship. It was dark and there was a certain amount of fog.

Tom saw all the passengers and crew away. There were about six boats and, what with the fog and the smoke from the burning *Persephone*, there was a great deal of confusion. When Tom came up from his cabin carrying the ship's papers, the boat which had been waiting alongside for him had drifted off. There on deck was Arabella, still in her crinoline, who had missed the last boat because she had gone down to her cabin to get the jewel case she had forgotten in the first alarm.

Luckily there was one small deck boat still unlaunched, and Tom lowered this and the two bundled into it. But by this time the rest of the boats had drifted away into the fog and the smoke and they couldn't make contact with them.

"Tom," said my grandfather, "wasn't unduly worried. No skipper likes to lose his ship, of course. But he knew that the *Persephone* was old and that Sparkman was well insured. Port au Prince was only five days off. Given reasonable weather Tom knew that he could make it. He'd been brought up in small boats. He hoisted the small sail and set a course for Port au Prince. The first mate was with the other boats and Tom knew that he was a capable man."

It was coldish during the night and Arabella had only a thin shawl to cover her shoulders. Tom gave her his jacket and they sat close together for warmth. When daylight came it soon grew hot and she left off the jacket and moved to the bows. There was no sign of the other boats.

At midday a sudden squall, ripping down out of nowhere, slashed the small boat's sail to ribbons and carried it away before Tom could do anything. However, there were thread and sailmaker's needles in the boat's locker as well as food and water — old Sparkman insisted fanatically on all boats being properly provisioned — so Tom took off his shirt and began to fashion a sail. But he hadn't got enough material.

In the most delicate way possible he asked Arabella if she were prepared to make some contribution to the sail. After some

23

consideration she made him keep his eyes sternward and produced one of her many undergarments.

My grandfather chuckled. "But they had bad luck, my boy. At least, if that's what you like to call it when you're stranded in a small boat with the one woman in the world you love. You see, during the next three days, one squall after another whipped down out of a clear blue sky and tore away the sail. And each time — since Tom was now reduced to his trousers — he had to turn sternward while Arabella produced more and more sail material from under her crinoline.

In the end, of course, the crinoline went as well. There they sat, the two of them, reduced to the barest minimum of clothes while above them the crinoline sail bellied in the breeze. And at night, when it turned cold, they huddled together for warmth. Many an hour Arabella slept in Tom's arms while he kept watch and steered. Tom was in heaven.

"Yes," said my grandfather. "Tom was a happy man. All day he sat looking at his lovely Arabella seeing far more of her than he had ever seen before ... her corn-coloured hair floating in the breeze, her lovely arms and shoulders now a golden tan under the sun. And at night she slept in his arms.

"He was very kind to her, of course. Treated her like a princess. Wouldn't let her do a thing. Not that there was much to do except steer, and while he did this he told her how much he loved her. And — by dint of repetition — her blue eyes softened a little. He had a way, you know. But even so they didn't soften all that much. She was a girl of great spirit. Then, just before sunset on the evening of the sixth day, they saw land ahead."

It was then, sitting there half naked the two of them, that Tom told Arabella that he wouldn't sail into Port au Prince direct. He'd go down the coast a little, land at some quiet beach and get clothes for her. To sail into a crowded harbour as they were would have ruined Arabella's reputation for life.

"Tom said to her," explained my grandfather, " 'Your reputation is to me the most precious thing in the world. But before I go ashore I ask you for the last time to marry me — and this time I know what your answer will be.' For a moment little points of ice danced in Arabella's eyes. 'You mean, Captain Ancaster, that if I don't say yes, it will be easy for you to be indiscreet about our voyage. The world will use its imagination ... The price of your silence is marriage.'

"Tom looked at her for a moment and then, his face hard with angry lines, he said, 'I see, Miss Arabella, that I have been mistaken about you — and you about me. I withdraw my last proposal.'

"From then on he never said another word. He took the boat down the coast, landed, left Arabella hidden in an empty cabin, and walked into Port au Prince. He was back within a few hours with a complete outfit of clothes for her. In silence he delivered her safely to her father's house, where he learned that the other boats had arrived safely the day before."

"And he never married her?" I asked.

"You're a fool, my boy. You know nothing about women," said my grandfather. "When Tom was summoned to see Sparkman the next day, Arabella met him in the hallway, put her arms around him, kissed him, begged his forgiveness for her words, and said that she had told her father that they were to be married. But when he went in to see Sparkman, the old man — after questioning him about the fire — said, 'I hear you and Arabella want to get married. Yes, yes, she's told me about the sail going and using her clothes. A secret, of course, between us. But I can't give my consent.

" 'I had great hopes for you, Ancaster, but this affair has decided me. You've slipped up, you know. If you married Arabella and finally took over this business, you would make other and larger slips. I've always insisted on all my ships' boats being properly provisioned and stocked. You should have had a spare sail in the locker. Why didn't you?'

"And Tom," said my grandfather, "looked at the old man and said quietly, 'Love is a strange thing, sir. For some people it can only bloom when all pride and finery are jettisoned so that they see each other as they are. Between ourselves, sir — and I would like it always to be our secret — I did have a spare sail in the locker.' "

COPY COUPON

If you had seen Miss Duncall getting off the train at Cannon Street station each morning — or for that matter getting on it each evening — you would not have had much trouble in placing her. She was obviously a private secretary and, equally obviously, not a high-powered, well-groomed one. She was thirty-five and looked older than that.

Usually she wore a dark suit with a white blouse, and she had a slightly old-fashioned taste in hats; but she was neat and trim and had a friendly face and warm, grey eyes. She was not the kind of girl to make a man look twice — though it must be said that an hour or two in a beauty parlour and a little more imagination on her part could easily have altered this state of affairs. She had no near relatives and she lived in rooms in a suburb. She spent a fortnight each year at a farm in Devon, the same farm every year, went to the theatre once a month, and for most of the rest of her spare time read romantic novels.

She would have been most indignant if anyone had suggested that she was either lonely or unhappy. She was content with her life, even though there were a lot of things she could have wished for — and one thing in particular.

The one thing in particular was Mr Eardy. Mr Eardy was ten years older than Miss Duncall, and he was her boss. Mr Eardy ran a wholesale office stationery firm in the city, and you would have thought that it would be a very nice little business indeed. But it wasn't. There was something about Mr Eardy that just didn't attract success. He could have had a sole concesion to sell ice-creams on a Mediterranean beach and, for no apparent reason except that he was Mr Eardy, would not have made a success of it.

Not that Mr Eardy was a failure. He wasn't. But he just wasn't a success. And it was nothing to do with his personality. He was a pleasant little man, plumpish, going a little bald and inclined to take rather a long time over his lunch. In the two years Miss Duncall had been with him he had never lost his temper or been anything but polite to her. He had a small flat at Richmond and once, when he had been ill, Miss Duncall had gone there to take some letters from him.

26

All the time he had dictated to her, sitting up in bed with his green and white flannel pyjamas showing at the neck of a dressing gown that should have been sent to a jumble sale years before, Miss Duncall's fingers itched to get to work on the flat and tidy and clean it up.

Miss Duncall was in love with Mr Eardy. And Mr Eardy? Well, as far as Miss Duncall could see, she had practically no existence for him outside the office. But it would be wrong to suppose they had never met outside the office. They had — on the occasion that Mr Eardy had backed a Derby winner and had won twenty-five pounds.

Mr Eardy was a passionate gambler. Passionate but careful. He had far too great a respect for money to over-reach himself. For Mr Eardy the excitement of a gamble lay not in the amount of the stake but in the gamble itself. On the occasion of his Derby win, quite out of the blue he had said, "Miss Duncall, a day by the sea would do us both good. I suggest Brighton."

And to Brighton they had gone in a hired car, and had finished up by getting back to London in the evening in time to go to the theatre and have supper afterwards. Throughout the whole day they had talked mostly of office affairs and had been excessively polite to each other. It was a day that Miss Duncall remembered vividly. Every moment had been a joy to her. It wasn't until he said goodnight to her at the end of the day that he had told her about the Derby win, and he had explained, "When you have luck, Miss Duncall, the best thing in the world is to share it with someone."

After that Miss Duncall had become interested in Mr Eardy's gambling. She found it, she had to admit, a little odd in him because he was a religious man. She herself had been brought up to think that gambling was the ruin of many a fine home. She was impressed by Mr Eardy's moderation.

It wasn't long before Mr Eardy discovered that Miss Duncall was interested in his love of gambling. When times in the office were slack, which was often, he would explain about form and the bloodlines in horses. In addition to horses, Mr Eardy did the football pools. He did them each week, venturing a modest five shillings. He would fill out a form each Thursday, make a copy of it which he put in one of the desk pigeon-holes, and then post his coupon on his way to lunch.

Now Miss Duncall, who shrank at the thought of bookmakers and placing bets, was fascinated by the pools system and, unknown to Mr Eardy, she applied to the same pools firm and began to do the pools. Since she knew nothing about football and was convinced that Mr Eardy knew everything, she would wait until he went off to lunchand then take his copy from his desk and enter up his forecasts on her own coupon and post it off.

Her faith in Mr Eardy was not shaken when for months she never won a penny. Each week she copied his forcast and sent it off and every Saturday she sat by the radio and checked the results and shook her head at their bad luck. And then, one Saturday at the beginning of February, instead of shaking her head as the results came through, her face broke into a delighted smile. For the first time in months Mr Eardy had forecast all his results correctly.

On Monday morning Miss Duncall went to the office happy with the thought that at last Mr Eardy had won something. But she said nothing to him because she did not want him to know that she had been taking his forecast from his desk and copying it. Mr Eardy, she thought, showed no signs of elation. Nor did he on the Tuesday or Wednesday. Miss Duncall just assumed that he hadn't checked his results that week.

On the Thursday morning Miss Duncall had the shock of her life. She had always stated on the pools form that she wanted any winnings to be treated without publicity. A letter came for her and out tumbled a cheque for twenty thousand pounds and a charming letter of congratulation from the pools firm.

Miss Duncall travelled to work in a dream. But curiously enough she was happier for Mr Eardy than for herself — for anything she had won he must have won.

But in the office Mr Eardy showed not the slightest sign of elation. When Miss Duncall took him his tea at half past eleven on a Thursday morning, she usually found him filling up his week's pools form. This morning he was just sitting, his chair tipped back and his eyes on a patch of grey sky visible through the window.

Unable to control her excitement any longer and trying to find a way to bring the subject up with him, Miss Duncall said, "Don't forget, sir — it's your morning for doing the pools."

Mr Eardy's eyes came round to her and he shook his head ruefully. "Not this morning, Miss Duncall."

"Why not, sir?"

Mr Eardy began to stir his tea slowly and, his eyes still on her, said, "Do you know what happened to me last week, Miss Duncall? I filled out my pools form and got a correct forecast. For the first time ever. And do you know what the winnings are this week for that forecast? Twenty thousand pounds. Just think of it! Twenty thousand pounds!"

"But that's wonderful, Mr Eardy."

"Yes, it would have been, wouldn't it? Twenty thousand pounds, Miss Duncall. Do you know what I would have done with it? I would have sold up this business — not that I would have got much for it. And I would have bought a small farm in Devon or Somerset. I've always wanted that, you know — a small farm and someone to share it with me. Someone ..." He began to blush a little but his eyes still met hers frankly. "Someone like you, Miss Duncall. Oh, please don't be offended." As he spoke his hand had taken Miss Duncall's.

When she replied her voice was tremulous with emotion.

"Oh, Mr Eardy. That would be wonderful. And really, I'm not offended. In fact the money doesn't matter ..."

Mr Eardy jumped to his feet and put his hands on her shoulders. "You mean — you would marry me, just as things are?"

"But of course. You see, I have some money of my own. Enough, I think, to manage that farm."

Miss Duncall was given no chance to say more for the moment. She was in his arms and he was kissing her and through her bliss she was thinking that she could never tell him how she came to have a little money of her own — not the truth, anyway. Hadn't he said, when you have luck the best thing in the world is to share it with someone — someone you loved?

But later she said, "Tell me, why didn't you post your coupon, Mr Eardy?"

"Harold."

"Why, Harold?"

He smiled, his arm round her shoulder. "I was going to but when I got outside I suddenly remembered that last week was the first week of Lent. I'm a bit old-fashioned, you know, Miss Duncall —"

"Helen."

29

"Helen. Yes, a bit old-fashioned. I believe in giving something up for Lent. Something you really enjoy. And with me it's my little flutter on the horses and the pools. So I didn't post my coupon."

THROUGH THE WALL

Nearly every afternoon around four, I have a bath bun and a cup of tea in a café near our office in Fenchurch Street. It's not much of a café now, but in the old days — I mean 'way back — I'm told there used to be a famous London coffee house on the site. Nothing famous about it now — just a café with people like myself dodging in and out for a break from work.

And mostly they are the same people. A regular clientele, you might say. You get to know faces, even get to miss faces — but you don't get to know the people. All you get is a few disjointed facts that you pick up now and again.

Take Fingleton, for instance. I don't know his first name. Just Fingleton. Usually he's there on Mondays, Wednesdays, and Thursdays. Always sits down at my table if there's a free seat, and we talk for about five minutes and then go our different ways. I don't know what Fingleton does, and he doesn't know what I do. But I know what he thinks about our Test cricketers, about football, about politics, about TV programs — he's mad about Westerns. He's about forty, going bald, and doesn't look too healthy. But he's got a nice smile and always has a cheery word for the waitress. Nice chap.

Then there's Haverstock. I don't know his first name either. Just Haverstock. He's a tall, lean-faced, almost aristocratic-looking chap, if you know what I mean. Looks as though he's seen better days. Faded elegance would be it, maybe. He comes in about once a week but never on any regular day. Just pops up, and then sometimes you don't see him for a month, and then he's in again week after week.

What do I know about Haverstock? Not much. He doesn't normally talk a lot — always seems to be brooding about something. I know one thing, though. He's mad about London. Knows all its history, knows all the churches and who built them — why, he can name you all the Lord Mayors right back and back! And he's good on coins, too. Fingleton brought in some old coin he'd found and Haverstock said right away it was a George the First shilling or something.

31

Well, now and again the three of us come together — it's just chance, about twenty or thirty times a year. Over the past five years. We're old friends. City types. And we don't know a damned thing about one another. Makes you think, doesn't it?

But I like it in a way. There's nothing spoils friendship like getting too friendly. In another five years, I suppose, we might have got round to knowing each other's first names. Might have. Because, you see, I haven't seen either of them for a year, but I remember very clearly the last time I saw them.

June, it was. Fingleton was with me, having bath buns and tea, and in walks Haverstock, drooping and faded and looking very harassed. He orders and drinks half his cup without saying a word.

I said, "You look under the weather, old boy."

Haverstock nodded. "Am a bit. Think I need a holiday. Too much rushing about. Beginning to get me down. It's a strain. Your nerves begin to go. Get irritable. Not yourself any longer. A man can only take so much of it. I tell you, sometimes I begin to wonder."

"Wonder? About what?" asked Fingleton.

"Just wonder. Life doesn't seem real any longer."

"You do need a holiday, old boy," I said.

"Undoubtedly. But I won't get one just yet. Have to have a nervous breakdown first ..." He paused, holding half a bath bun aloft, and chewed thoughtfully; then he said, "You ever thought much about London — about all the people in it?"

"What about them?" asked Fingleton.

"They scare me. So many of them. Hundreds and thousands, going round and round, popping into offices, dashing for trains. Thousands and thousands of strangers. None of them really interested in any of the others. Nobody knowing anybody else. You know, you get so that you don't even look at other people. If you did, you'd get some shocks — that is, if you really looked at other people."

"You do need a holiday," I said.

"I don't think so. Not for this kind of thing. Nobody would believe it."

"Believe what?" asked Fingleton.

"What happens if you watch people in London. I know."

I looked at Fingleton and winked. "What do you know, old boy?" Poor old Haverstock was really under the weather.

"I know that a great many of them aren't what they seem to be. I've been studying it lately. And once you begin, you can't stop. I'll tell you something. I was walking down from St. Paul's to Ludgate Circus the other day and there was a man in front of me. Just an ordinary chap — so ordinary that at first I didn't really take him in. And then I did. Don't ask me why. I just said to myself that he was a human being like me and not just a face. So I — well, I sort of concentrated on him. I walked behind him, across the Circus and up Fleet Street. And do you know what?"

"You tell us," I said.

"A little way up Fleet Street he crossed a side road ahead of me and a post office van turned into the side road blocking him from me for a few seconds. Only a few seconds. But when the van passed and I looked — he was gone. Gone!"

"Popped into a doorway, I'd say."

"There wasn't one. He just went like that." Haverstock snapped his fingers. "All right, you can smile. But since then I've got into the habit of watching people. Nobody does it in London. No time for other people. But I've watched them. The other day it was a young girl by the Bank. You know what she did?"

"Disappeared up a lamp-post," said Fingleton.

Haverstock didn't seem to mind our laughter. "You aren't far out. She went over a pedestrian crossing just ahead of me. I'd been following her for some time. She stepped onto the pavement in the middle of the crowd and went slap through the wall of the Bank. Slap through. And not a soul noticed."

"Oh, come off it," said Fingleton, "You really need a doctor."

"Or an oculist," I said.

"I don't need either," said Haverstock, a bit stiffly this time. "It happened, and I think I know why."

"Why?"

Haverstock took a deep breath. "Well, my theory is this. London is full of people. Thousands of them, and not all of them are living. It's full of ghosts. People in the past who have worked here, given their lives to this place, got so attached to it, the whole of their lives just one long habit of being in London, of being part of it … Well, when they die they can't escape. They come back. People come back, don't they? To the places they were attached to? I tell you London is full of ghosts."

33

"How many have you seen?" asked Fingleton sceptically. "Just one man and one girl. There could have been a perfectly logical explanation. The man jumped on a bus or other people got between you and him and you missed him. And the girl — well, she couldn't go through a wall. She just got mixed up in the crowd, or you had a few bilious spots in front of your eyes for a moment and some trick of the light made you imagine it."

Haverstock shook his head. "I may have plenty on my mind with the way business is going — but I'm still seeing straight. I tell you, I saw those two. And since then I've seen others. I tell you, I've got into the habit of watching people now and the damndest things happen. I've even seen it at night, when I've been working late. A man ahead of you in a deserted street. You're only five paces behind. You turn a corner after him and — he's gone. Once you begin to watch people it happens — it keeps happening. And I tell you, it's not a good habit to get into. I wish I could stop myself now. But I can't. I'll be walking down a street and suddenly someone ahead of me attracts my attention — and I know it's going to happen again."

Fingleton laughed, and stood up.

"Haverstock, old man," he said, "you need a holiday and a check-up with your doctor. But it's a good yarn, and I entirely agree with you that we're all strangers. Well, see you sometime."

He went toward the door, and Haverstock and I watched him go out.

Haverstock said, "Don't you believe me? Damn it, I'm not seeing things."

"Well ..." I didn't really know what to say. "I suppose it's a ..."

I stopped talking, my hand still in my pocket where I had begun to fiddle for change to pay my bill. My eyes were on Fingleton who had just gone out of the café door.

He crossed the street. I saw him clearly through the window.

He stepped onto the pavement and walked across it — and went straight through the brick wall opposite.

The shock hit me like a blow. I turned and looked at Haverstock. He was staring out of the window, too, and had clearly been watching Fingleton.

34

Haverstock gave me one look and then got up and went. I haven't seen him since.

Or Fingleton.

FLIGHT OF FANCY

It's a common adult misconception that a child's world is a curious mixture of fancy and reality, that the boundary between the bizarre and plain fact is a shadowy one. Nothing could be more untrue. A child's world is a sharp, vivid one where everything exists in a bold, unquestionable vitality. It's the adult who dreams, who believes in fairy tales and miracles — and he has to do this to escape now and then from life. Children don't need to escape: life to them is still sunrise and full of glowing colours.

Take a typical example of this misconception — Mr. and Mrs. Charles Letterworth. Charles was a country solicitor, about 40, level-headed, intelligent, and with no reason to suppose that be was anything else but an enlightened father. And as a solicitor he felt that he was well qualified to distinguish fact front fiction.

His wife, Phyllis, was a good-looking, capable woman who took her full share of the activities of the village in which they lived. She was a good pianist and before her marriage had been the assistant editor of a woman's magazine. Now, she was more than content to run a home in the country and to devote all her love to her husband and to their one son, Peter, aged eight.

Peter was the problem child — not a very big problem, but one which had began to worry both Phyllis and Charles Letterworth. From a very early age both of them had cultivated the habit of telling Peter a bedtime story, and then later had directed his first reading efforts to children's books which they carefully selected.

Peter loved the stories he was told and read and they were very real to him. If they hadn't been real to him they would have been bad stories. But now, with Peter eight years old, the Letterworths were worried because they felt that the love of fantasy and fairy stories which they had inculcated in Peter was spilling over into a distressing tendency on his part to tell lies.

One evening, over their before-dinner drink, Phyllis said to Charles, "He came home late this afternoon with six beautiful peaches. I know they must have come from the Rectory garden because that's the only place around here that grows peaches. And I know he must have stolen them because I telephoned the Rector —

he knows every peach on his tree — and he confirmed that six were missing."

Charles sipped his sherry thoughtfully, and then asked, "What did Peter say?"

"That he was walking down the road by the Rectory when a man stepped out of the bushes and gave the six peaches to him."

"Just that?"

"No. He was carrying a jam jar full of tiddlers — I mean Peter was — that he'd caught up at the millpond. The man said that a jam jar was no place for fish to live and if he'd put them back in the stream he would give Peter the six peaches. But that's not all. Peter says the man was wearing a sort of fireman's helmet and carrying a sword — a kind of knight without a horse. Anyway, Peter put the fish back and took the peaches.

"It's all just an elaborate cover-up for stealing the peaches, isn't it? This knight-in-armour business? We've had that one before."

"I'm afraid so. Charles, I'm worried about it. It's natural enough for a child to steal a few apples or peaches. And in a way it's natural for them to tell a few fibs — but not this fantastic rigmarole! If he goes on like this and we don't check it, he'll grow up thinking he can always get away with it — and *then* we shall leave a real problem."

"Well, it could be that he's one of those boys who's going to have to learn the difference between the truth and a lie the hard way."

"Oh, no, Charles — you couldn't!"

"I could and I will — if it's necessary. My father gave me one beating in my life. I've never forgotten it and I learned a valuable lesson. You talk to him and tell him that if he ever tells another lie like this one I shall have to punish him. What happened about the peaches?"

"The Rector was sweet — he begged me to keep them."

Well, Peter got his talking to, and nothing happened to upset Charles and Phyllis as far as the boy was concerned for three weeks. Then one evening Charles got home from his office to be greeted by his wife:

"Charles, I've sent Peter up to bed without dinner. I'm afraid you're going to have to — well, it's just that the whole thing has got beyond me."

37

"What happened? Not this knight with a sword again?"

"I'm afraid so. And much more. This time the knight was riding a white horse. And he had jewels and —"

"Take it easy." Charles put a hand on his wife's shoulder. "Let's have it straight from the beginning."

His wife sat down and gave him the story as it, had been told to her by Peter. The boy had arrived home about five o'clock and he was wet through. He said that he had been up at the millpond, fishing again. Like his father, he was a keen fisherman — though he used only a hickory stick with an old piece of string tied to the tip and a sixpenny hook with a worm on it.

Father and son often fished together in the millpond. It was the ambition — not only of Charles but of every other fishing man in the village — to catch an old cannibal trout that lived in the pond. The trout was referred to locally as Old Wary and on the few occasions he had been hooked he had got away. But leaning over the mill bridge, Charles and Peter had often watched him slithering in the green depths below.

Well, Peter — Phyllis continued — was fishing from the, bank with a worm when he had got a bite. After a few moments he realized that it was Old Wary, and in the ensuing fight Peter had slipped and fallen into the water; but he had eventually managed to land Old Wary on the bank.

"What — on that rotten bit of string and his hickory stick? Nonsense! Couldn't be done!"

"He insists on it. But, of course, it's just a story to excuse his falling in and his fishing up there alone. He knows it's forbidden unless someone is with him."

"Of course … Why, if he'd caught old Wary he would have brought him home. The whole village would have wanted to see the fish and he knows it."

"That's the point. He says that he was going to bring the fish home. But just at that moment down to the stream comes this knight of his, and this time riding on a white horse. From what I can make out from Peter, this knight of his looked down at the fish and said that it was wicked to pull it from the stream where it was so happy. He said that if the fish wasn't thrown back it would die, and once a thing was dead it could never come back to life. Not all the money and jewels in the world could bring it back to life."

38

The knight, Phyllis went on, had then pulled from his pockets a great handful of jewels — rings and strings of pearls — and had tossed them into the stream. He had said that you could fill the stream with riches and still the fish could never be brought back to life once it had died.

"And Peter threw the fish back?" said Charles.

"Yes. And the knight on his white horse rode off waving his sword and with his helmet shining in the sun."

"He falls into the stream when fishing alone. Then, instead of admitting it frankly, he tells this whopper. I'll just have to deal with him. He's got to learn that an unpleasant fact can't be hidden by a fantastic fib."

Charles left the room; but he didn't go up to Peter right away. He went out and, strolled down to the village pub. He hated the thought of beating his boy and he didn't mind admitting to himself that he wanted to put off the evil hour by having a quiet drink and thinking over what he would say to Peter. The beating by itself — he knew from experience with his own father — was nothing unless the words that went with it were the right ones.

The pub was empty except for the landlord who served Charles with a large whiskey and then, leaning his elbows on the counter, said, "You look a bit down, Mr. Letterworth. Tell you a story that'll cheer you up. Know that foreign sort of butler they've got up at the Hall? Well, he did a flit this afternoon. Took a lot of Her Ladyship's jewels, and what's more — this'll give you a laugh — pinched one of His Lordship's hunters. That white mare.

"Off he goes, as mad as a March hare — wearing an old helmet of His Lordship's and wavin' a cavalry sword. Caught him over near Roydall about an hour ago. Mad as a hatter, it seems. Once or twice before, apparently, he's had those fits and gone off — always with a helmet and a sword. Kept it quiet they did — you know how soft-hearted Her Ladyship is. But this time, because of the hunter and the jewels, they put the police on him.

"Funny world, ain't it? If I'd met a bloke coming down the street wearing a helmet, ridin' a white horse, wavin' a sword, and chucking jewels around, I'd say it just wasn't true. Wouldn't you?"

Charles looked up smiling. "Not any more I wouldn't."

39

SANCTUARY FOR THE GENERAL

Major-General Sir Henry Braithwaite, K.B.E., C.B., D.S.O., M.C., known to his friends as Galloper, was having breakfast. *The Times* was propped against the coffee pot, and he was spreading marmalade on his toast with a thin-bladed pygmy hunting-knife which had come from the Ituri forests of the Congo. The May morning sunshine streamed through the mullioned windows of the breakfast-room of Lambertill Hall and there was a lingering aroma of kippers in the air. Kippers were Sir Henry's favourite breakfast food, and the two he had just finished were the first he had had in eighteen months.

The General was a fine, intimidating figure of a man. His fair hair was now thin and whitening, his blue eyes clear and frank against a suntanned complexion, and his beaked Roman nose presided over a fierce cavalry moustache. As the chairman of a committee, a justice of the peace, or a judge at a horse show, the General stood no nonsense from anyone. In fact, it would have been difficult for the General to remember the last time he had ever stood any nonsense from anyone in any walk of life. He snorted now at a piece of nonsense in the third leader and threw the paper to the floor just as his man, Murch, came into the room. Murch — once Trooper Murch — was the only indoor servant the General could afford.

"Timms, sir, is outside, sir, waiting to see you," said Murch.

"Timms? What does he want? I said I'd walk round with him this afternoon."

"He said something about the bulldozer, sir."

"The bulldozer? What are you talking about, Murch?"

"The bulldozer, sir."

"I heard you the first time. But what bulldozer?"

"I wouldn't know, sir. I don't meddle with the outside things. I've enough to do in here, sir."

The General cocked an eye at Murch, but wisely did not pursue this aspect of the conversation. Murch, gloomy, sardonic, but utterly faithful to the General, had been agitating in his own peculiarly devious way for two years to get the General to buy him a washing-up machine. Actually, the General might have been able, with a little pinching here and there, to run to a washing-up machine. But the real snag was that there was no electricity at Lambertill Hall.

"Excellent kippers, Murch. Excellent. If it's possible, your touch has improved while I've been away."

The General got up and went out, a tall well-built figure in shooting-jacket and breeches. Timms was waiting for him in the driveway, a shotgun crooked under his arm. Timms — once Trooper Timms — was the outside man, the gardener and game-keeper of two-hundred-odd acres — all that was now left of the Lambertill estate, the rest having long been sold to pay taxes.

These two hundred acres of wild heath, woodland, and marsh, running down to the North Sea, the General had turned into a bird sanctuary. Ornithology was the passion of the General's life. The only shooting that was ever done on the Lambertill Estate was of vermin, like rats and squirrels, that plagued the nesting birds. After a lifetime of warfare in various parts of the globe the General had become, in his own way, a man of peace.

"Morning, Timms. What the devil's all this about a bulldozer?"

"Morning, General. It's the bulldozer for the new road, sir. Thought you'd like to know they're making a start."

"Bulldozer? What road?"

"The new road, sir. Coming in by the quarry copse they are, off the Lamindon road."

"What the devil is this?" The General's blue eyes glinted fiercely. "My gold-crested wrens nest every year in the pines down there. Come on, man — let's get to the bottom of this. New road! Has someone gone mad while I've been away?"

The General strode off, followed by Timms.

Half a mile from the Hall, where the country road to the small town of Lamindon bordered the estate, there was a clump of pines at the side of an old quarry. As they approached, the General saw that a man was busy pulling up a length of chestnut paling while another man sat in the driving-seat of a bulldozer waiting to move in. Somebody, the General noticed in fury, had stuck a row of surveyor's red-and-white stakes across the ground running from the quarry into the estate.

Seeing the man busy on his chestnut paling, the General took the gun from Timms and fired a couple of shots into the air, well

41

above the man's head. The man sat back, surprised, into the ditch and was still sitting there when the General arrived.

"What the devil do you two think you're doing?" roared the General, and Timms, hearing the thunder in his voice, was taken back to his days in tanks when the General had commanded an Armoured Division.

The man pulled himself from the ditch and said petulantly, "You shot at me!"

"Don't talk damned nonsense, man! I shot over you. What's going on here?"

The man on the bulldozer took a cigarette from his mouth and said amiably, "The new road, General. Cuts right across to Lambertill beach and then on to Sandfields. We've just got to make an entrance for the lorries and other stuff to get in. Nice to see you back, General."

For a moment the General looked in silence from one man to the other. Like a good tactician he made a quick appreciation of the situation, and arrived at two conclusions: one, nobody was taking down his fence and driving a bulldozer through his land and, two, this outrage had to be tackled at source.

He snorted and said commandingly, "Timms, stay here. If either of them lays a hand on that fence or tries to drive that machine in — shoot."

"Yes, sir."

"I'll go and find out about this."

The amiable man on the bulldozer nodded. "That's right, General. But it won't do you any good. All signed and sealed, it is."

"Then it will all be unsigned and unsealed, my man!"

The General turned and strode off, fuming. His land, his birds, all to be mucked up with a new road to Lambertill beach and Sandfields when there was already a perfectly good — if longer — road running round the back of the estate!

Half an hour later he drove into Lamindon in his open, vintage Phantom II Rolls-Royce, intent on visiting his solicitor. As he parked his car in front of the Town Hall, a young constable came up to him.

"Sorry, sir — you can't park your car there. New regulation. Reserved for the Mayor and council members."

This was the last straw to the General.

"Listen, young man," he said, "I've been parking my car there for years, and before I had a car I parked my bicycle there, and my grandfather parked his penny-farthing there before me. Give the Mayor my compliments and tell him and the town council to sue me and be damned! Now, don't delay me any longer!"

He strode off to the offices of Wench, Welton, and Barnhill, Solicitors and Commissioners for Oaths, leaving the young constable open-mouthed.

A few minutes later he crashed into Harvey Wench's office. Harvey, a pleasant, competent young man, had served under the General in World War II, and now handled all the General's legal affairs.

"Good morning, General. You're just in time for a glass of sherry."

"I don't want sherry, young feller. I want an explanation. What have you been up to, you nincompoop? What is all this about a new road to Sandfields through my place? A new road — right across one of the finest stretches of country around here. Disturbing my bittern and shrike! What have you been doing while I've been away?"

Harvey waited for the gale to subside and then said patiently, "But, General — I wrote to you about this while you were away. It's part of the new county development scheme for Lambertill beach and Sandfields. The Minister has given his consent — after a public hearing. Surely you remember? You sent me a telegram telling me to go ahead. It only cuts across a corner of your land and you get — I must say this — very handsome compensation."

"I don't care a fig for the compensation. I'm thinking of my bird sanctuary. And what letter? What telegram? I didn't get any letters in the Ituri forest. D'you think there's a postal service in the middle of the Congo? And the only telegram I sent you was about those shares of mine you were fussing over before I left — those property holdings. I changed my mind and wired you before I went up-country — GO THROUGH WITH PROPERTY DEAL MENTIONED BY YOU."

Harvey's face fell. "Oh dear — there's been a ghastly mix-up. I thought your telegram was an answer to my letter."

"I don't care what you or anyone else thought! Just tell the county people to haul off their bulldozers. I'm not selling any more

43

of my land. Anyone who wants to go to Lambertill beach can go round by the old road, or across the estate bridlepath. I've never stopped people coming on my place so long as they behave themselves. Encouraged 'em, in fact. But I'm not having any damn road with cars whizzing about, disturbing the birds. In no time they'll be setting up hot-dog stands and lord knows what. Turning the foreshore into a lido or some damn rot like that. People want a sanctuary as much as the birds — and that's what Lambertill is going to remain. A sanctuary."

Harvey shook his head. "It can't be done, General. The whole thing is signed and sealed. You know what these official bodies are like."

"Have you had the cheque for the sale?"

"No."

"Then that's it. I won't accept it. Just tell them the whole thing is off. Phone the County Surveyor now and tell him to recall that bulldozer. Tell him Timms and I will shoot anyone who tries to come in."

"But, General —"

"No buts. Get cracking." The General turned on his heels and left the room before Harvey could say anything.

He went back to his car, and the young constable on duty, watching him drive off, decided that it might be better not to report the parking offence.

That weekend Harvey carne over to Lambertill Hall to report progress.

"I'm sorry, General," he said. "But there is nothing we can do. They say they're not responsible for the mistake and they must go ahead."

"What?" The General's roar echoed round the library. "Go ahead, must they? We'll see about that!"

Harvey recognised that the General was now in one of his 'Galloper' moods. In other words, when surrounded by the enemy, he was prepared to give his charger its head, draw his sword and, backed by stalwart troopers, cut his way out.

"I'm afraid we're too late," said Harvey nervously. "The Minister has given his authority for this thing, the County Council are all on their toes ready to go, Government grants have been made —"

"And the whole thing has been a mistake. I've never given permission and I never will!" exploded the General.

" There was a public inquiry into the affair. They say that you should have objected then."

"How could I ? Don't be a blithering idiot! I was in Africa and knew nothing. All they have to do is to see that and cancel everything. But not them. They're so tied up in red tape that once a thing has been settled they've no idea how to unsettle it."

"They don't want to, that's why. And anyway, they can always make a compulsory purchase order against you."

"What? Force me to sell my own land? What is this country — a concentration camp? Don't people have any rights to their own property?"

"Not if they stand in the way of beneficial developments."

"Beneficial! What's beneficial about a new road when there's a perfectly adequate old one? What's beneficial about turning a quiet beach into a jam-packed lido? And what about the hundreds of people who take civilised pleasure in walking round the sanctuary watching the birds, eh? And what about the birds, eh? What about them? Are they going to like it? Do you think any self-respecting godwit, Sandwich tern, or spotted flycatcher is going to nest around here if this road goes through?"

"There isn't a thing I can do, General."

The General snorted and fixed himself a whisky and soda. "Harvey, that's just the spineless kind of thing that you would say. Tie a piece of red tape round something and it becomes sacred to you. If a thing is wrong, it's wrong, and they've got to put it right. I'll make them!"

"What can you do?" Harvey asked.

"Fight them! Right the way up to the top. Already I've told the Chairman of the County Council Highways Committee that he will never be invited to dinner here again, and that his fishing syndicate's lease on Lambertill lake will not be renewed next year unless all work is suspended for a month."

"He agreed?"

"He had to. I've got a month's respite. I'm going to London on Monday to see Bunty Haggerty."

"Who's he?"

"Bunty? He used to be a pimple-faced squirt at Charterhouse with me. Used to make him do my Latin and Greek prep for me. Odd blighter — never played games. Always poking round old churches, digging up flint arrowheads. Mad on archaeology. At the moment he happens to be the Right Hon. Bernard Willoughby Haggerty, M.P., member of Her Majesty's Cabinet and Minister of Rural Transport and Civil Aviation. Don't ask me why. He probably thinks a Sopwith Camel was something with four legs, and he's the fool who's given permission for roads to be plastered all over the country in places where people don't want 'em."

And on Monday the General motored to London and went to see the Right Hon. Bernard Willoughby Haggerty.

It was no tender reunion. Bunty, a short, plump, and rather pompous man, was polite — hiding successfully a long-ingrained nervousness of the Galloper's pugnacious manner — but he could offer no balm. The scheme was all settled and must go through.

"Bunty," fumed the General, "I'm warning you that I'm not taking no for an answer. This is going higher. Where's the P.M.? I'll see him."

"The Prime Minister is in Paris. He doesn't get back for, a week. There's nothing you can do, General. Believe me."

"We'll see. How the devil would you like someone driving a road across your ground?"

"If it were in the national interest I should submit gracefully."

"Then you'd be a fool. National interest. That's what they always say when they have no real argument. Right — then I'll go above the P.M."

"I should like to know where."

"Then I'll tell you." And the General mentioned the name of a Very High Royal Person indeed.

For a moment Bunty's face paled. "You know him?"

"As good as. Damn it, I nearly married his wife, didn't I? When I was a subaltern, Poppy and I were very good friends. But she decided in the end to plump for being a Duchess rather than a camp follower to a warrior. Don't blame her."

And to Poppy the General went. The Duchess, no longer the slim, giggling debutante whom the General had once known, was charmed to see him. He sat in her boudoir and they had tea together and talked over old times, and then they were joined by her husband, the Duke, and to the two of them the General put his problem.

"Bird sanctuary, eh?" said the Duke. "No shootin'?"

"No, sir. Only with a camera."

"Dull, what?"

"Of course it isn't," said the Duchess. "It's much harder to get a good picture of a marsh harrier feeding its young than it is to knock down a couple of high-flying pheasants."

"That so? Interestin'."

"You must do something for Galloper," said Poppy.

"True, my love," said the Duke. "But so far as I can see it's birds, peace, and quiet against a new road. Not much argument there. Some like birds and peace and quiet, and just as many like new roads and noisy beaches. I mean, if they wanted to knock down St. Paul's and make a road through, or Nelson's Column, then there'd be something to work on. But I'll try. Going to Paris tomorrow. Could have a word with the P. M."

Two days later the General had a telephone call from the Duchess to say that the Duke's plea had been sympathetically heard by the Prime Minister, but very diplomatically turned down. This was a departmental matter and not of sufficient national importance to warrant interference from him at this late stage.

Many another man would have taken this as final. But not Galloper Braithwaite. He brooded on the matter for a whole day, and then in the evening wandered into the kitchen where Murch was washing up. For some time the General said nothing, but he absently took a dish towel and began to dry the plates. Murch gave him a gloomy look and waited, silently.

After a time the General said, " Murch, how much does one of these washer things cost?"

"About sixty pounds, I think, sir."

"I see."

"There would be the installing of the electricity as well, sir."

"How much?"

"About three hundred pounds, I understand, sir."

"I see."

"Not that I am not content with things as they are, sir. But it is a bit hard on the hands. Always was prone to chapping, sir, as you know. Early morning stables was a nightmare to me sometimes, sir."

47

"Call it four hundred pounds altogether, eh?" The General grunted. "Well, we might manage it, Murch. We might — if you cooperate."

"Cooperate, sir?"

"In a little scheme. Could be dangerous, though. I mean, it calls for courage and discretion."

"Illegal, sir?" Murch knew the General.

"In a way."

"I'd be delighted, sir. Anything to save my hands, sir."

"Good — then get Timms in here and we'll fix it up."

"Timms, sir?"

"It's an outside as well as an inside job. And I shall need you both to come to London with me the day after tomorrow. A road across my land, eh? Scaring my birds, mucking the place up for decent folk on the beach — I'll show them!"

Two evenings later, at six o'clock, the General walked into the bar of his club, not far from Claridge's Hotel in Brook Street, and found, as he knew he would, Sir James Knowland, the millionaire proprietor of the *Daily World*, contemplating his sixth whisky of the day.

"Evening, Jimmy."

"Evening, Galloper. Whisky?"

"Thank you."

They drank in silence for a while, and then the General said casually, "Tell me, Jimmy — how much would your paper pay for a real scoop?"

"Depends, Galloper. Real big stuff no limit."

"Indeed. Well, four hundred quid is all a friend of mine wants. First-class story, too. You could just catch the press tonight with it. Absolutely exclusive."

"What is it?"

"Not so fast, Jimmy. First — the money would have to be paid to me, and the whole thing is in strict confidence. After all, the fellow's doing me a great service."

"You sure there is a friend, Galloper? "

"If that's your attitude, I can take this somewhere else."

Sir James Knowland shook his head. "Four hundred to you. Strict confidence. If the story is good."

"Read this."

The General handed over a typewritten sheet to Sir James. Sir James read it, whistled, and broke into a great smile. "No stopping you, is there, Galloper? O. K. Strict confidence. Money in the mail to you tonight. Sorry, I must hurry."

The next morning, at the breakfast tables of those fortunate enough to subscribe to the *Daily World*, the news broke. Within a few hours the wires all over the country and the world were humming with it.

The Right Hon. Bernard Willoughby Haggerty, M.P., Minister of Rural Transport and Civil Aviation, had been kidnapped, changing for dinner at his house.

An anonymous communication received by the editor of the *Daily World* announced that the kidnapper, an admirer of Major-General Sir Henry Braithwaite, and also a passionate ornithologist and campaigner for the preservation of the rural beauties of England, meant to hold on to the Right Hon. Bernard Willoughby Haggerty until the scheme to drive a road through the Lambertill Bird Sanctuary was withdrawn. If the scheme were not withdrawn the Right Hon. Bernard Willoughby Haggerty would never see the light of day again.

The repercussions were many and rapid. The Lambertill road scheme, which had been only of local interest, suddenly became of international interest. The legion of societies for and against planning, for and against new roads, for and against wild life and rural preservation, and so on, went into action with a spate of letters to the press. The manservant of Bunty Haggerty, besieged by reporters, could only say that his master had gone up to change for dinner and had never come down. His black tie was still laid out on the bed, but the rest of his evening clothes had disappeared with him.

Nearer home the exchanges were sharper. Harvey Wench rang the General and told him that he would never get away with it. The General replied, "Don't know what you're talking about. Nothing to do with me. Damned nice of whoever it was."

The Duchess, staying at a nearby country house, telephoned and said, "Galloper, how like you. So dashing! But it won't do any good. Wrap him up and send him back."

The General thanked her for her interest and invited her to dinner the following weekend.

The Chief Constable of the County, prodded from Scotland Yard — they in turn prodded by the Prime Minister — arrived at Lambertill Hall with a search warrant.

"Hope you haven't got this chap around, Galloper. Look bad for you if I turn him up."

The General, who hunted regularly with the Chief Constable, gave him a glass of sherry and told him to have a good look round. The Chief Constable and his men departed without finding any trace of the Right Hon. Bernard Willoughby Haggerty.

And there the matter was. A member of Her Majesty's Cabinet missing, an ultimatum issued, the preliminary work for the road halted, and the General, Murch, and Timms going about their business with cheerful unconcern. Yes, even Murch was cheerful, for the General had written to the local contractors for an estimate for installing electricity in the Hall, and Murch was happily collecting brochures of washing-up machines.

Bunty Haggerty was, of course, at Lambertill. His kidnapping had been a matter of no great difficulty to three seasoned campaigners like the General, Murch, and Timms.

Some half a mile from the Hall there was a large range of dunes, a favourite nesting place for sand martins. Here — during World War II — an anti-aircraft gun had been sited. The gun was now long gone, but there remained an old ammunition store which the gunners had dug into the sandy side of the dune and lined with logs. The stout door to the store was now overgrown with a wilderness of tamarisk and gorse bushes and it would have needed the eyes of a hawk to spot it. Here the General visited Bunty each evening after nightfall, accompanied by Timms carrying food and drink for the beleaguered member of Her Majesty's Cabinet.

The General was sitting with him now, an old cavalry sword resting across his knees in case Bunty tried to escape. Timms had retired. Bunty, in evening dress less a black tie, watching the glint of hurricane lamplight on the sword, was openly nervous, but also pugnacious.

"You'll never get away with this, Galloper. You've really put yourself in the soup."

"Pooh and bah!" said the General. "They'll come round. Every day you stay here, work piles up at your Ministry. They'll have to come round."

"And if they don't?"

"I'll send them first your right ear and then your left. Or the other way round if you prefer it."

"You can't play ducks and drakes with the Government like this. You're mad."

"If the Government can play ducks and drakes with me and my bird sanctuary, I can do the same with them. Trouble with people these days is they won't stand up for their rights against you red-tape-ridden bureaucrats."

The General stood up to go. As he did so, his eye fell on a spade at the far end of the store where the logs holding back the sand had rotted away. Fresh sand lay over the ground. The General cocked an eye at Bunty. "Been digging, I see."

Bunty replied belligerently, "I've a right to try and escape."

"Certainly," said the General. "Duty of every officer when taken prisoner. But you'll never make it that way. Two hundred yards of solid dune. But it's healthy exercise. Good night."

For four days the mystery of the missing Cabinet member obsessed the nation, and for four days various members of the Government and as many of the War Office — old friends of Galloper's, and all convinced that he was holding Bunty Haggerty somewhere — applied pressure in their different ways to make him see sense.

To all of them the General made substantially the same reply. "If the Lambertill road goes through you'll have to get a new Minister. With thousands of others, I fought for this country in its hour of need. I'm not standing by now to see it desecrated by a lot of bureaucratic morons who don't know how to change their minds. They're the kind who've made the dodo and the Cornish red-legged chough extinct, and wouldn't turn a hair if the golden eagle went the same way. Sanctuary is what we need for birds and men."

But in the end a pressure was brought on the General which he could not resist. When the Duchess came to dinner with him that weekend, the Duke came as well. They ate in the long dining-hall by candlelight, and when the port was served Poppy refused to leave the men.

The Duke sipped his glass, held it up to the candlelight, and with that air of wellbeing which comes from good port only, said, " I'm not sure. Could be a Gould-Campbell, 1927."

51

"Cockburn, '27," said the General. "Only six dozen left. See me out."

The Duke nodded and then said, " Talkin' of seein' you out … might not be long, head on a block, what, and all that — if you hang on to Bunty Haggerty."

Poppy, smiling graciously at the General, said, "You've got to turn him loose, Galloper."

" 'Fraid so," said the Duke. "Do it now, no repercussions. Whole matter smoothed over. But the P.M. is worried. Government being made to look foolish. Laughin' stock of the world. Bad for international relations, you know."

The General circulated the port, watched the Duke refill his glass, and realised that he was being given an order; and the order was coming from a man who, in the strict military sense, was his commander.

Sadly, thinking of his birds and of the lovely stretch of wild country which so many people enjoyed in peace and quiet, all now to be changed, he said, "Of course, sir."

Poppy, sorry for him, said, "It was a good try, Galloper, my dear. But these are modern times … people don't understand."

"Better get him now," said the Duke. "I'll talk to him and see he doesn't get any ideas about making trouble. Where is he?"

The General told him, and the Duke and Duchess, since it was a fine evening, decided to walk to the dunes with the General. They found Bunty Haggerty at the back of the store, digging away by the light of two hurricane lamps. For a while he was unaware of their presence.

"Tryin' to escape?" queried the Duke.

The General shook his head. "More for exercise than anything else, sir. Keeps him fit. He's been doing it ever since I put him here. Hey, Bunty!"

The Right Hon. Bernard Willoughby Haggerty turned and, recognising the Duke and Duchess, came forward to be greeted by them. He looked dirty, dishevelled, and exhausted, but there was a curious glint in his eyes.

"Sentence remitted," said the General. "You're free. Come back to the Hall and clean up. Give you a comfortable bed for the night."

"No hard feelings," said the Duke. "Forget and forgive."

"That's an order, of course," said Poppy, winking at the General. "Forget and forgive."

"Forget!" cried Bunty, finding his voice. "I'll never forget my time here as long as I live! The world is going to know about it!"

"Now — come, come!" soothed the Duke.

"No, you come, sir," said Bunty. "This way. Come and look at this."

He started back to the end of the store where he had dug into the wall about ten feet, opening a great space. He held up a hurricane lamp and his eyes shone. "Look — it must be! Archaeologists have been looking for it for years. But always round the present site of Lamindon. But it's been here all the time, five miles away."

Under the lamplight they saw a spread of tessellated pavement, in its centre an intricate blue and green dolphin design surrounded by men and women in ancient clothes. The colours glowed richly under the soft lamplight.

"Roman mosaic," said Poppy. "How lovely!"

"It's the lost Roman city of Laminium!" cried Bunty. "Floor of a villa. There must be others, all hidden under these dunes. A great archaeological treasure. It could be bigger than Verulamium —"

"And you're going to drive a road through the lot," said the General sourly. "New road comes right across these dunes."

"New road!" Bunty almost shrieked. "Vandalism! There's going to be no new road across here! We can't destroy the country's antiquities. I'd be blackballed from the Athenaeum, thrown out of every archaeological society in the country if I allowed it. I'll fight it tooth and nail."

"Absolutely," said the Duke. "Like driving a road through St. Paul's. No one would stand for it."

The General looked at Poppy, and she said quietly, " No road."

"No road," said the General, and he was thinking happily of the splendid stretches of Roman paving which would be brought into the sunlight. Here, in the heart of his sanctuary, people would be able to enjoy the beauties of a past civilisation and the pleasures of bird wild-life. There would be some disturbance while the old villas were being uncovered, but that would soon pass. He would keep an eye on things ... A car park down on the Lamindon road and then a quiet walk along the bridlepath to ancient Laminium ...

53

"Don't just stand there," said the Duke to the General, cutting in on his reverie. "Go and get a couple more spades. I want to see what the rest of the floor looks like."

"Yes, sir," said the General.

"And bring the rest of that Cockburn 1927 with you. Going to be thirsty work. Haggerty and I will be needing it."

VINTAGE VENDETTA

The auctioneer let the buzz of excitement around the room subside. Then, in a fat, satisfied voice, he said, "One thousand pounds I am offered. One thousand pounds, ladies and gentlemen. Any advance on one thousand pounds?"

He looked across m the direction of Professor Patrick Walter Fitzharris, M.Sc., F.I.M., F.R.Ae.S., now retired, but at one time Professor of Industrial Metallurgy at Midland University, member of the Council of United Kingdom Metals Association, and author of *Principles of Foundry Metallurgy*, which, while not as exciting as *Gone with the Wind*, in the last twenty years had sold almost as many copies throughout the world. The Professor glared back at the auctioneer, all his Irish blood stirred up.

The Professor was a short, wiry, jockey-sized man of about sixty, grey-haired, and with bright blue eyes now sparkling with frustration. At his side sat Lydia Annette Fitzharris, his daughter, blonde, with softer blue eyes than her father, a willowy figure in tweeds, the air about her faintly touched with the fragrance of Miss Dior. She put a hand on his arm and said, "Control yourself, Daddy — you can't afford it."

"Control myself, is it," growled the Professor, his anger emphasising his native brogue. "I want it and I'm going to have it. What would a man be if he only bought the things he could afford?"

"Solvent," said Lydia crisply.

"Then it's no way to live," said the Professor.

"One thousand pounds — for the first time," began the auctioneer. "One thousand pounds — for the second time —"

"Guineas!" barked the Professor.

Lydia raised her eyes to heaven and gave up.

"Thank you, Professor," said the auctioneer, smiling, and then announced to the company, "One thousand guineas I am offered. One thousand guineas ..." He went off into his patter and his head was now turned to a distant part of the saleroom.

While he did so, the Professor said in a fierce whisper to Lydia, "Who's bidding against me? Thought this would be a snip."

"I don't know," said Lydia. "But if you're not careful you'll be pushed right over your limit."

"By Saint Patrick and the Holy Spectrum," snorted the Professor, "there's no limit to a thing like this!"

Lydia smiled to herself at her father's passion.

"Some day," she said, "you must tell me what the Holy Spectrum is."

"One thousand five hundred," said a voice from the far back of the crowd. Swiftly though he screwed his head round to try and catch a glimpse of the other bidder, the Professor could not pick him out. Only Lydia at his side frowned sharply as she thought she now recognised the voice.

"Somebody else must have discovered it, too," groaned the Professor, then with a belligerent look at the auctioneer, he called, "Guineas!"

And the object of the rising emotion and frustration in the Professor's breast? Well, unless you happen to share his particular type of passion, you have little hope of understanding fully.

The Professor was a lover of old motor cars. He was a member of the Veteran Car Club and the Vintage Sports-Car Club. He already owned a 1906 Wolseley-Siddeley tourer, and still used a 1927 Alfa-Romeo 22/90 to drive himself about in. There is a distinction, of course, between Veteran, Edwardian, and Vintage in the motor-car world. Veteran cars must have been manufactured not later than 1904, then follows the Edwardian period from 1905 to 1916, and the Vintage cars run from 1919 to 1930.

The thing which the Professor thought that he alone had spotted in the list of contents for sale at the auction of an old country-house was a motor car. Under the heading *Miscellaneous* — immediately after *Outside Equipment and Garden Tools and Furniture* — it had been catalogued simply as *Sunbeam car, good running order*.

But when the Professor had come to view it before the sale he had realised with considerable excitement that this was the understatement of the year. The car was in fact a 1913 Sunbeam 12/16, a tourer, which to any lover of old motor cars was like an art dealer coming across an unknown Utrillo in an outhouse.

The auctioneer caught the Professor's eye as a voice from the back of the room said, "One thousand eight hundred pounds."

"Guineas!" the Professor fired back.

The auctioneer smiled happily. But there was no happiness in the Professor. To his increasing annoyance and frustration the unknown bidder outbid him all the way up to two thousand pounds. When the bidding reached that point even the Professor sadly recognised his limit, and the car was knocked down to the other man for that amount.

The Professor, fuming with disappointment and anger, stumped out of the room, got into his vintage Alfa-Romeo, and drove off, quite forgetting that his daughter, Lydia, had accompanied him to the sale.

Lydia did not mind this, however. She was used to her father's moods. She went out of the house, threading through the auction crowd, to the garage at the bottom of the drive. A young man was leaning against the door, eating a sandwich, a vacuum flask in one hand. He turned as she came up and grinned at her. He was a tallish young man of about twenty-five, blue-eyed, fair-haired, and his brown face was marked with a suspicion of freckles. His name was Richard Denby and he had met Lydia once before.

"Hi, there," he said pleasantly. "Cold day. Like a cup of coffee?"

Before Lydia could reply, he had filled a cup for her. He handed it to her with a little bow.

Lydia said, "We've met before, haven't we?"

"Lord," said Richard, "did I make such little impression? Yes, at the Hunt Ball two weeks ago. We had three dances together, and you only drank lemonade. As a matter of fact, I fell hopelessly in love with you. I still am, madly. Would you mind if I asked you to marry me?"

Lydia frowned. He was an attractive young man, and she remembered him well, but at the moment love and marriage were far from her mind.

"Why were you bidding for the Sunbeam?" she asked.

"This baby?" He nodded into the garage where the old car sat, its brass and bodywork sadly in need of polish. "Beauty, isn't she? Bit of work on her and you won't recognise her. Actually I wasn't bidding for her. Can't afford that kind of money. If I could, I'd be putting it into my business."

"Business?"

"You remember — I told you about it at the dance. I've just started a garage in Rivervale. Mean to have a string of them all over the country in the next ten years. No, in this, I was a kind of agent."

"Bidding for someone else?"

"Yes."

"Who?"

"Is it etiquette to say?"

"To hell with etiquette," said Lydia sharply. She could produce something of her father's directness when necessary.

"Just as you like," said Richard. "I'd break any rule for you. It was for Sir John Coddinstone. Told me to go up to three thousand if necessary."

"Sir John Coddinstone!" Lydia's eyes widened.

"Why'd you say it like that?"

A wry smile played about Lydia's lovely lips. "That's nothing to the way my father would say it if he knew. He and Sir John would cheerfully murder one another to get possession of, say, a Mercedes-Simplex."

"They're scarce."

"I know. There isn't much I don't know about cars."

"Excellent. You know, I've a theory that women should become car salesmen, I mean, saleswomen. After all, who decides on the family car, really? Why, the woman. You can have a job in my place, if you like —"

"You don't waste any time, do you? Which do I get first, the job or marriage?" Lydia smiled. "Anyway, you'd have to ask my father about marriage and when he knows about this —"

"You'll tell him?"

"Why not? You don't want things made easy for you, do you?"

"For you — no obstacle counts. Would you like a sandwich to go with that coffee?"

"No, thanks." Lydia put the cup down and walked away, but as she went she was smiling to herself. Of course, a girl would prefer to be wooed more romantically, but there was something refreshing about Richard Denby's directness, and she liked the way his fair hair strayed a little untidily over his forehead.

Actually Lydia did not have to tell her father about the way Sir John had outbid him at the auction. Sir John Coddinstone, C.B.E., J.P., head of Coddinstone Steel Products and a handful of other

58

companies, now semi-retired, told the Professor himself. He arrived at the Professor's house, which was a few miles outside Rivervale, that evening at half past six in time to be given, reluctantly, a whisky and soda.

Between the Professor and Sir John there had existed, since the time they both went to the same public school together, a curious love-hate relationship. They were both quick-tempered men with wills of their own. At school they had competed fiercely for the last place in the cricket and rugby teams and for election to various exclusive societies. As young men they had fallen in love with the same girls and in retirement they had by chance settled in the same part of the country. The Professor, whose metallurgical researches had contributed to Sir John's business successes, had the pure scientist's indifference to wealth. He just regretted that his chosen field of research had brought him so much in contact with Sir John.

Life had never missed a chance to keep the feud going between them. It was typical of life that it had made them both keen Veteran car enthusiasts. Sir John owned and still used a 1928 Alvis 12/50, front-wheel drive, and could not have been more scathing of the merits of the Professor's Alfa-Romeo.

"Well, Fitzy!" bellowed Sir John, "I see you've done it again. Blast you!" Sir John was a large, jovial-faced, fleshy man, the same age as the Professor, and he habitually addressed everyone as though half a gale were blowing. His voice now made the glasses on the sideboard ring and the Professor wince.

"Done what? And don't shout at me. I'm not deaf, even if you are."

"I'm not deaf! And you know what I mean. I've just had a letter from the Secretary of Knight's saying I've been blackballed again. That's the fifth time."

Knight's Club, of which the Professor was not only a member, but also Chairman of the House Committee, was an exclusive London club, where one could eat well and in comfort, where the port was excellent, and the stakes at cards as high as one cared to make them. It had long been Sir John's ambition to become a member.

The Professor shrugged his shoulders. "Somebody there doesn't like you. Plain. Why keep on trying?"

"Somebody!" Sir John took a turn up the room, paused at the sideboard and helped himself to another whisky and soda. "It's you, Fitzy! Every time my name comes up you slip in the one black ball that counts against me. Damn rotten show. After all, you've got nothing against me really. I mean, not from a club point of view."

"No?" The Professor lit his pipe unhurriedly. Then he went on, "A club, Coddy, is a place where a man goes to relax, to be with friends, to enjoy himself. He doesn't want to meet people there he doesn't want to meet. Whole idea of a club. Now take you — ever since you turned up at school with me, I've been runnin' into you all over the place. Turn a damned corner, no matter where, and there you are. But not at Knight's. I can't tell you what a joy it is, Coddy, to be certain that every time I go through the door of Knight's I know that you can't follow."

"Dashed unfriendly. Just because I squeezed you out of the rugger team, and then that young girl —"

"Old history, Coddy. Go away, there's a good chap."

"I will. But I'll tell you something — I got the Secretary's letter this morning. If I'd been elected, I was going to let you alone to bid for that 1913 Sunbeam just out of gratitude. But not when I learnt you'd done it again. Yes — don't look so pop-eyed, Fitzy — it was me bidding against you, through a young feller called Denby who's just started a garage in Rivervale. Any time you care to withdraw your objection to me bein' a member of Knight's, Fitzy — then you can have the Sunbeam for two thousand pounds."

"Bribery — by all that's holy!" The Professor was on his feet.

"Prejudice!" Sir John smacked his empty whisky glass down. As they glared at each other, Lydia came into the room.

"What are you two shouting about?" she asked.

"Shouting?" Sir John looked amazed. "Just thanking your Father for the drink, my dear. Must be on my way, eh? Good night, all."

When Sir John had gone, the Professor poured himself a stiff drink, muttering to himself as he did so.

Lydia said, "There's a young man to see you."

"Send him away."

"I can't. He wants to ask you for permission to marry me."

The Professor spun round. "Marriage! Is this, the day of my greatest tribulation, the time to be introducing such a subject? It's more like murder, I feel!"

Lydia smiled. Before her father could say more she went to the door and opened it.

"Come in," she called.

Richard Denby entered the room.

"Daddy," said Lydia softly, her eyes on Richard, "this is Mr. Richard Denby, who wants —"

"What name?" the Professor roared.

The door closed as Lydia retired. Richard, wincing a little at the roar, stood his ground by the door.

"Denby, sir."

"Denby — the garage bloke?"

"Yes, sir."

Perhaps it would be as well to draw a veil over the rest of the very short and mostly one-sided conversation. A few minutes later, as Richard left the house, Lydia appeared from the bushes at the drive side and, chuckling, said, "Don't talk now." She slid into the spare seat of his car and went on, "Just drive to Rivervale. The Rose and Crown. You look quite pale and you need a drink."

"For a moment," said Richard faintly, "I thought I'd never get out of there without needing medical attention. I had no idea that a Professor knew such language!"

"They pick it up over the years from their students," said Lydia.

"You've no idea what he asked Saint Patrick to do to me — with the help of something called the Holy Spectrum."

"Drive, don't talk," said Lydia. "I'm thinking."

Richard didn't know it, and some men much older and more experienced than he would not have known it, but Lydia had just uttered the most dangerous words a woman can utter. *Don't talk, I'm thinking.* They always mean that a woman wants something and is determined to have it.

When Lydia returned home that evening, the Professor was waiting up for her. Lydia was late because the restorative drink she had offered to Richard had been reciprocated by an invitation to have dinner with him. She came in, humming gently to herself, her blue eyes sparkling.

61

The Professor greeted her without preliminaries. "Damned cheek of that young man, Denby."

"Oh, I don't know," Lydia said airily.

"Well, I do. Damn it — he bid against me for the Sunbeam on Coddy's behalf!"

"He's got nice manners and I like the way his hair goes."

"By all Ireland's green acres, girl! You don't marry a man for that kind of thing. Besides, you can't marry until you're twenty-one without my permission. And anyway, twenty-one or not, if you married a man who had caused so much sorrow to your old father, I'd turn you out —"

"Into the snow?"

"Depends on the time of year. And I'd cut you off without a shilling."

Lydia smiled. "You've been reading some old-fashioned novels, Daddy."

"They're the best. Anyway, what I mean is you wouldn't get my blessing."

Lydia nodded gravely. "That's different. I'd like your blessing. Why are you so prejudiced against him? You don't know him. It's just like you are with Sir John. He's a nice man but you persist in fighting each other, when you'd both like to be friends."

"Friends — with that awful money-grubber Coddy! Heaven Forbid! And I forbid you to see this young man."

"Sorry, Daddy, I can't refuse to see my employer."

"Employer!"

"Yes. He's given me a job as a car saleswoman. I start tomorrow morning. Could I interest you in a new car?"

"No, you couldn't!" barked the Professor. "There hasn't been a decent car made since 1930! The only car you can interest me in is that 1913 Sunbeam Coddy stole from me."

"Stole?"

"As good as."

"I heard him offering to let you have it for two thousand if you'd support his application for Knight's."

"By the Holy Spectrum — you think I'd do that! Bandy a club membership about for money! Coddy must be losing his grip to imagine such a thing. Sacrilege!"

62

For a moment Lydia was silent, thinking. Then she said softly, "No two women would behave as stupidly as you two men. Something must be done about it ... Yes" — there was a faraway look in her eyes — "something must be done."

"I don't know what you're talking about, girl. Go to bed. And you're not to take that job, and you're not to encourage that young Denby."

Lydia came over, kissed the top of his head, and then went off to bed.

The next morning she was at the Denby Garage ready for work at nine o'clock. That the labour relations between employee and employer were going to be amicable was established by the fact that her new boss greeted her in the office with a kiss which Lydia showed no signs of not enjoying.

Nevertheless, as they parted, she said, "One thing I will not do is marry without Daddy's blessing. At the moment, as far as you are concerned, Richard, I might as well enter a nunnery. We must think of something to make him change his mind."

"Of course," said Richard, his eyes on her full of love and admiration, knowing that he had never seen nor ever would see anyone half as lovely. "You do that."

This last sentence proved Richard to be a young man of good sense. He knew that changing men's minds was woman's work.

A week later, on a Monday morning, Professor Patrick Walter Fitzharris received in the post a typewritten letter from Sir John Coddinstone which read as follows:

> *Dear Fitzy,*
> *It was unpardonable of me, of course, to offer to sell you my 1913 Sunbeam in return for your support to my next application for membership of Knight's. I can only put down my lapse of good taste to stress of emotion.*
> *However, since I know the strong sporting instincts and the love of a wager which distinguishes all members of Knight's, I am prepared to issue the following challenge. I will race you over a thirty-mile course on Wivenhoe Beach, cars to be used — my 1913 Sunbeam against your 1906 Wolseley-Siddeley. Stakes — if you*

win, you take the Sunbeam, and if I win, you support my
application to Knight's.

Yours,

Coddy

Surprisingly enough, Sir John Coddinstone also that morning received a letter from the Professor. It read:

> *Dear Coddy,*
> *I've been thinking about this club affair. The offer you made about Knight's and the Sunbeam was in pretty bad taste, even for you. But underneath I suppose you're not a bad old scout. Tell you what I'll do, I'll give you a sporting chance. I'll wager that in my Wolseley-Siddeley tourer I can beat you in your Sunbeam over a thirty-mile circuit on Wivenhoe Beach. Stakes — if you win, I'll support your application to Knight's, and if I win, I take the 1913 Sunbeam.*
> *Give me a ring before I change my mind.*
>
> > *Yours,*
> >
> > *Fitzy*

Within five minutes Sir John was on the telephone to the Professor.

"Well, Coddy?"

"Well, Fitzy?"

"My Sunbeam will leave your scrapheap miles behind."

"I doubt," said the Professor icily, "whether you'll even get that box of chair springs of yours to start. If you do, it'll break up with metal fatigue after a mile."

"I will meet you at Wivenhoe Beach this afternoon at two-thirty to agree a course."

"Do that."

At lunchtime that day the Professor told Lydia — who showed no surprise at the news — about the challenge, and finished, "I'll have to spend some time tuning up the engine, getting everything in racing trim. I wondered if you'd care to give me a hand — that is, if you can spare time from that, job of yours which I forbade you to take."

"I shall be glad to help, Daddy. And thank you for inquiring about the job. Yes, I'm doing very well there and I'm very happy in my work."

"You're as devious as your mother was at times," said the Professor. "And almost as good-looking." He smiled at her.

Meanwhile, at Sir John's house the same lunchtime, young Richard Denby was getting his briefing.

"I don't care what you've got on hand at your garage, my boy. Drop everything and get cracking on that Sunbeam. I want it in tiptop condition by next Monday for this race. Spare no expense. If I win, I might put up a little money for your next garage. Might, I said — it depends."

Later that afternoon, the Professor and Sir John met at the beach. Wivenhoe was a five-mile stretch of isolated sand, ideally formed to be the jousting place of these hard-bitten knights of the wheel. The two of them walked the bone-hard sand together, a stiff early spring breeze battering them. They agreed on a course four miles long with a post at each end for turning markers, and they settled for four complete laps.

From the top of the cliffs, Richard and Lydia watched the two men below. Richard, his arm round Lydia, said, "I still don't understand. Only one of them can be the winner. Either the Professor gets the Sunbeam or Sir John gets into the club. How does that help us?"

"You want to marry me, don't you?"

"Of course I do!"

"And you know I won't without my father's blessing. When the parson says, 'If any man can show just cause' — you know the bit — he's capable of jumping up and starting an argument."

"But I still don't understand how this race helps us."

"You will. Now listen and concentrate. What I want from you are two simple mathematical calculations."

Richard listened, his eyes widening, his admiration for Lydia increasing ...

So, for the next few days Richard and Sir John worked on the Sunbeam, tuning it up and grooming it into tiptop racing trim. Elsewhere, the Professor and Lydia did the same for the Wolseley-Siddeley.

65

Oddly enough, when the day of the race came, Lydia, pleading a headache, said she could not go to the race. She felt more like going to bed. She got the Wolseley-Siddeley out of the garage for her father, and he set off for the drive to the beach by himself. The moment he was gone, Lydia's migraine disappeared and she went off to the Denby Garage in Rivervale in the highest of good spirits.

When the Professor arrived at Wivenhoe, Sir John was already there, and with him was Richard Denby.

"Brought Denby along as starter. That all right by you, Fitzy?"

The Professor grunted.

The two cars were lined up alongside the starting post. The long stretch of sands ran smoothly towards the distant cliffs, and far out could be glimpsed the creaming breakers of the sea. A few seabirds wheeled round, crying, and a thin spring sun shone bleakly down. The cars, hoods down for racing, looked magnificent. The Wolseley-Siddeley, its green-and-red bodywork sparkling, was a little higher and older fashioned in line than the Sunbeam, whose cream-and-chocolate body gleamed as though it were glowing with some inner health. Brasswork dazzling the, eye, they made a magnificent pair.

The Professor pulled on an old motoring cap, donned goggles, and said, "Well, let's get started, and remember, Coddy — the chap who's ahead has the right to cut in. If you don't give way — then by Saint Patrick that's your funeral."

Sir John pulled on a woollen balaclava hat and goggles and said, "I'm not going to be behind at all, so there's no question of me giving way. Denby will count down from ten and then give us the starting gun."

Richard watched the two men climb into their cars. The engine notes increased a little and they sounded solid, throaty, ready to go.

He began to count. "Ten, nine, eight, seven ..." And as he did so, he hoped fervently that he had worked out correctly the little calculations Lydia had given him. If he'd made a mistake he knew there would be hell to pay from Lydia.

"Three, two, one —"

He fired the starting gun and the engine growls rose to a crescendo and the cars were away, their back wheels spinning for a moment on the hard sand.

It was a race which Richard was to remember with pleasure all his life. He, too, was a lover of old cars and here, on this lonely beach, to see this road-hardened pair, one from 1906 and the other from 1913, still full of power and fight, spurt away down the hard yellow sands, was an inspiring sight. They roared away from him, engines and gears whining as the drivers made their changes, their bodyworks flashing red and green, cream and chocolate, the stiff spring wind taking their exhaust fumes, and the sun sparkling on their brasswork. It was a wonderful moment.

Richard walked up the steeply sloping beach to a sandy bluff and pulled out his fieldglasses, training them on the cars.

A quarter of a mile from the start Richard saw that Sir John in the Sunbeam had drawn just ahead of the Professor in the Wolseley-Siddeley and, when he had a clear lead, he pulled over, dead in front of the Professor. At the post marking the turn for the first half-lap, Sir John hugged the corner too tight and went wide as he came round into the straight. The Professor, obviously doing some very quick gear changing, pulled sharply inside him and went ahead by about a length.

The two cars came roaring back up the course and Richard saw that the Sunbeam was again drawing ahead. But Sir John could not get enough lead this time to head the Professor and, with a hungry roar of engines, back wheels flinging up great sprays of sand, they took the turn at the end of the first lap abreast. A mile down the straight of the second lap, Sir John went into the lead and increased it by the time he came to the post. This time he cornered more carefully, holding his ground, and he came roaring up the back end of the lap with the Professor a good hundred yards behind him.

At the end of the third lap, Sir John had a lead of three hundred yards. As the Professor took the turning-post behind him, Richard saw him thumping at the steering-wheel with one hand as though he were a jockey whipping up his mount to greater speed.

Sir John went into the first half of the last lap well ahead. He took the far turn, his lead increasing, and came charging into the home stretch, the sun gleaming on the Sunbeam's brass and paintwork. Behind him came the Professor, bare-headed now for the wind had swept away his cap.

Then, a mile from home, it happened. Richard saw the Sunbeam suddenly lose speed and then slowly come to a halt. Sir John leapt out and raised the engine cover. As he did so, the Professor, his exultant shout carrying on the wind, one hand raised derisively at Sir John, swept by in the Wolseley-Siddeley. But a hundred yards beyond the Sunbeam the Wolseley-Siddeley, too, suddenly lost speed and finally came to a halt. The Professor leapt out, too, and his head was soon stuck into the engine.

Richard walked down towards them. By the time he reached them, both gentlemen had discovered their trouble and Sir John had joined the Professor.

"By the Holy Spectrum!" cried the Professor. "We've both run out of petrol. No race."

"We'll run it again tomorrow." said Sir John.

"Without petrol," said Richard, "you're both in trouble right now."

"Why?" demanded the Professor.

"Because," said Richard, "it'll be high tide in another hour." He nodded out across the sands where the breakers of the fast incoming tide had grown larger. "And even between the three of us we can't push these machines up the steep sand slope from the beach."

"But we must get the cars off the beach!" roared Sir John. "If the tide gets them, they'll be ruined. You're a garage man, get up to the coastguard station and phone your place for a towing vehicle. It can be here in twenty minutes."

Richard went up to the coastguard station and on his way he was congratulating himself on his mathematics. While Lydia and he had been working on their respective cars, they had drilled holes in the petrol tanks nicely and mathematically calculated in diameter, to ensure that there should be a wastage of petrol from the time they unplugged the holes when the cars started for the beach.

Half an hour later, with the tide now coming dangerously close, Lydia arrived, driving a towing vehicle from the garage. She roared down to the beach and drew up by Sir John and her father. She jumped down, a slim, smiling girl, the sky-blue overalls, with Denby's Garage in bright red letters across the front, matching the blue of her eyes.

"Get our cars out of here quickly!" cried her father.

Lydia shook her head and tossed the ignition keys of the towing vehicle in her hand. "Not so fast, Daddy. At Denby's we always like to settle the charge for rescue work before we begin."

"Damn the money, Lydia," snorted Sir John. "We'll pay what you ask."

"I know you will. But the job can't be done for cash. Now let's see ..." Lydia frowned and rubbed a hand thoughtfully across the fair brow.

"Hurry, Lydia," growled her father. "The tide's coming in fast."

Lydia pulled a sheet of paper from her pocket.

"You'll both have to sign the contract. Here's a pen. I'll read the terms for you. 'In return for salvaging the two cars the following is agreed. One, Professor Patrick Walter Fitzharris agrees to support Sir John Coddinstone in his application for membership of Knight's. And, two, the aforesaid Sir John agrees to sell his Sunbeam to the aforesaid Professor for two thousand pounds.'"

"Blackmail," protested the Professor.

"Extortion!" roared Sir John.

"Goodbye," said Lydia, and began to move towards her vehicle. Both men shouted together, "Agreed!"

Lydia came back, smiling, and this time she had her arm linked in Richard's. "Also," she said, "the aforesaid Professor agrees to give his permission and unqualified blessing to the marriage of Lydia Annette Fitzharris to Richard Cromwell Sylvester Denby."

"Is this a moment to waste time in idle talk of marriage?" cried the Professor.

"Give me that pen," said Sir John. He took the pen and the contract and signed it. Then he handed them to the Professor.

"Fitzy, old fish," he said, his grey eyes twinkling, "one way and another we've both been done — and by an absolute charmer. Better sign and look happy. Seem to remember that your wife's father didn't think much of you to begin with. But you turned out fairly all right. So will young Denby. How can he go wrong with a girl like Lydia to manage him? Sign."

The Professor raised the pen over the contract, looked from Richard to Lydia, and then, his blue eyes sparkling, grinned.

"Why not? But by Saint Patrick, there's going to be a court of inquiry about this petrol business. Something fishy there."

"Later," said Lydia, as he signed. "Just now we've got work to do. Come on, Richard, let's get these old crocks off the beach."

"Old crocks!" The voices of the Professor and Sir John were raised in a unanimous roar of indignation that drowned for a moment the noise of the breaking surf.

THE BALLERINA AND THE PIGS

When the question of sending Assistant Commissar Pyotr Danilov to England to buy pigs was discussed there was a difference of opinion. "He is too young. The English farmers would cheat him," said the President.

"He is twenty-eight and with a youthful countenance, I admit," said the Minister of Agriculture. "But he knows pigs, and his father was a peasant. He will make no bad bargains."

"English farmers have a drink called cider which is drunk the whole time a bargain is being made," said the Minister of Propaganda and Culture. "It would confuse his judgment."

"You forget we have a drink called vodka," said the Minister of Agriculture dryly. "Young Pyotr can drink even Commissar Androv, my deputy, under the table."

"Well …" The President hesitated. "In the last two years we have had five assistant commissars go West on such missions and they have never come back. It looks bad." He glanced across at the Head of the Secret Police. "What do you think?"

The Head of the Secret Police, who had been leafing through a decadent democratic magazine full of photographs of bathing beauties — lent him by the Minister of Propaganda and Culture — said finally: "Pyotr is a firm believer in our way of life and would never desert it. Moreover, he has a good head for drink and bargains. Let him go. Also, there is a delicate little matter which needs attention in England. He will make no trouble about it. Send him."

So Pyotr Danilov was sent to England. He spent a month in Somerset making purchases for his government. At the end of that month quite a few farmers respected his capacity for cider and his eye for a pig. And quite a few farmers' daughters tried to make him stay in England, for with his fair hair and blue eyes, a charming smile, and a well-built muscular body, Pyotr was a man to attract a girl's attention. They were wasting their time.

One farmer who, rashly egged on by his daughter, offered Pyotr a partnership if he wished to stay, regretted it. Pyotr sat up all night

70

with him, drank him out of cider, and when the dawn came was still demonstrating how good life was behind the Iron Curtain..

"Oi tell 'e," said the farmer afterwards, "Oi damned nearly went back with 'e. That there convincin' 'e was. Charm a bird off a tree, 'e could."

Two days before Pyotr was due to fly back with his consignment of pigs, a man joined him at the bar of the Castle Hotel in Taunton. He was a short, dark-looking man with a permanent twitch to his upper lip and an astonishing capacity for whisky acquired after two years' service in the London embassy of Pyotr's country. Pyotr knew him well for he was the commercial attaché who had arranged all his contacts and finances on this trip.

The man called for a whisky and when it came lifted the glass and said: "Bung ho!"

Pyotr frowned. He disapproved of the acquisition of foreign habits. "Is everything arranged for the flight back?" he asked.

"No hitch. One of our own planes comes in tomorrow and you go off the next day. Pigs for the People's Democracy. I've never flown with pigs. What do you do to keep 'em happy? Sing to them?"

"If they show any signs of restlessness," said Pyotr stiffly, "I inject sedatives."

"Needn't do it with this lot. Just unpack Nadia Mariac and get her to dance for them."

"I do not understand," said Pyotr, and he stroked the beginnings of a fair moustache which he was growing to give his face more sternness. Nadia Mariac had been a member of the State Ballet, but a year before she had defected from the company while on a European tour and had taken asylum in London.

"She'll be with you. In a packing case marked 'Antibiotics.' Drugged, of course. Our police boys picked her up four days ago at Brighton. Did you get to Brighton? Typical Western decadence ... I go there most weekends."

"You mean," said Pyotr offended, "that I am to take her back? And you tell me this in a public drinking place?"

"Where'd you want me to tell you? In church? All business is done in bars over here. You must know that."

"But this is a secret service matter. I'm here for pigs."

"Don't worry. The airport people will give no trouble. Just tip her out of the case when you're airborne and then hand her over when you touch down. It ought to be a hell of a trip. Snow storms all over Europe is the forecast."

He gazed into the distance over his glass. "Nadia Mariac ... What a lucky man you are! Now, I wouldn't mind going home if I had her company on the way."

"That is no way to talk, comrade," said Pyotr crossly.

"I wasn't talking. I was ruminating. She's a wonderful creature; like a naiad, like the dream of all the world. She's going to find it hard work in the salt mines. Still, I suppose she must be shown the error of her ways."

"She must. And many others, too," said Pyotr curtly. But as he left the bar he was thinking that they ought not to have done it. Each department, in a well-run state, should look after its own affairs. Pigs and ballet dancers didn't mix.

There were fifty pedigree pigs, mostly young sows and boars, and one enormous sow due to farrow in a few days. For this last Pyotr had developed an extraordinary affection and respect. He had bought her from a best-selling author who ran a pig farm for tax evasion purposes, and she was a champion. From her loins, thought Pyotr, would spring a race of pigs that would enrich the impoverished strain of his own country.

Lady Chatterley was her pedigree name. "Give her love," the author-owner had said, "she thrives on it. It breaks my heart to part with her, but for good red gold I would sell my mother."

"She shall have every attention," said Pyotr, who had fallen in love with her on the spot. She was the size of a walrus, but not so good-looking, and with an endearing habit of charging her pen wall down and going berserk if not fed on time.

During the first fifteen minutes of being airborne Pyotr had his hands full of the pigs, and particularly of Lady Chatterley. They all showed signs of being annoyed at this unusual procedure.

Pyotr walked up and down between the crates and stalls that had been fitted into the fuselage, and he talked to his charges in a calming, comforting voice. Gradually the restlessness disappeared from them.

Carl and Ugo, the two pilots who had come over with the plane, glanced back and watched this performance with amusement. Between them was a large earthenware jar of cider, a parting present from the embassy's commercial attaché and, unknown to them,

72

laced with whisky. Lacing cider with whisky is like putting a match to gunpowder, only rather slower in effect.

"Sing to them," called Carl.

"Let Nadia out," added Ugo. "She will dance for them."

"Your duty is to pilot and navigate this machine," said Pyotr coming up the catwalk to them. "Attend to it! The woman will not be released until we are well over the sea. We might yet have to make an emergency landing."

"He thinks of everything," said Ugo.

"I remember Nadia in Swan Lake," said Carl. "Like thistledown. I have had her picture over my bed ever since."

"With twenty others," said Ugo. He reached for the cider jug, but Carl beat him to it.

Pyotr went back to Lady Chatterley. She lay on her side and sneered at him. He gave her an apple and she ate it, blowing long sighs through her nose. Above her, through the fuselage window, he could see the piled winter clouds, and far below, the grey edge of the sea tilting over the shrinking lip of the land.

Half an hour later he went to the tail of the plane where a large wooden case was stored. It was stamped all over: EXPORT ONLY, ANTIBIOTICS. KEEP AWAY FROM DAMP.

Ugo came up behind him and handed him a hammer and a chisel. "We're well over the sea."

Pyotr began to work on the case. He got the top off and between them they tipped the crate on to its side. Beautifully packed, Nadia Mariac came out like a Christmas present, untouched, unblemished, fresh and lovely, and sleeping peacefully.

"It'll be half an hour before she comes round," said Ugo.

"And in a filthy mood," called Carl.

Pyotr scarcely heard them. He was looking down at the figure of Nadia Mariac. Ugo had slipped a couple of rugs under her and she lay with one cheek resting on her hand. She was beautiful, with the longest lashes and the shapeliest legs Pyotr had ever seen. What a pity that so beautiful and talented a creature should have been politically so misguided! She had done his country a lot of harm when she had deserted the State Ballet. It was good, Pyotr thought, that now the Minister of Propaganda and Culture would be able to announce that she had returned of her own free will, disgusted with the western world.

He reached down and pulled her rumpled skirt lower over one of the loveliest knees he had ever seen.

An hour after take-off they were running into very bad weather.

"If it gets any worse," said Carl to Pyotr, "maybe we should land at Vienna."

"We go straight through," said Pyotr. "The sooner I get the pigs back the better."

"And Nadia?" asked Ugo.

"The pigs are my chief concern," said Pyotr stiffly. "We need them to improve our blood strain. Basically, we are an agricultural country. Our industry is growing — but to give it strength it must be supported by agriculture. In these pigs lie the health and vitality we need for the future. Why the police should go to all this trouble to get back this misguided ballet dancer, I can't think. She has been corrupted by the West. Like all artists, she is unstable and a liability, incapable of appreciating the glorious future which awaits us if we all dedicate ourselves to the simple, human truths of pure socialism."

"Oh, shut up! " said a voice.

The three men looked round. Nadia Mariac had come up behind them. Tall, dark and slim, she was frowning at them.

Ugo smiled. "Mademoiselle," he said, "I have long been an admirer of yours. I trust you slept well, and I assure you that, for my part, you could have stayed for ever free — I mean, in the West."

"Me, too," said Carl.

"I strongly disapprove of such talk!" snapped Pyotr, and he stroked his incipient moustache and looked stern.

"I'm sure you do," said Nadia. "I've met your kind before. You've swallowed the bait, the hook and a good length of line. That pig speech of yours was just too pompous, and you've no idea how silly you look when you try to be stern." She nodded at the jug which Carl was raising. "What's that?"

"Cider, mademoiselle."

Nadia took the jug and drank deeply.

"It is advisable to be careful with that," said Pyotr. "It is very strong."

"It's what I needed. A drink and a cigarette."

"Allow me." Ugo was on his feet with his case out.

"Certainly not," said Pyotr. "The smoke will upset my pigs. I cannot think why people find it necessary to drug themselves with tobacco."

"The People's Democracy finds drugs very useful at times," said Nadia.

"You will oblige me, mademoiselle," said Pyotr, "by keeping to the rear part of this machine and not talking with the pilots."

She looked at him for a moment, then turned and went back to her crate.

An hour later and the weather was worse. They were flying in cloud, fighting a headwind and swift showers of sleet and snow.

Carl said, "We ought to come down at Vienna to refuel."

Pyotr said, "You have plenty of petrol."

Ugo said, "But bucking this headwind will use it up. We ought to refuel. Besides, Vienna is a beautiful city."

"Very beautiful," said Nadia from her seat on the packing case. "I have danced there twice. We could take the Commissar Danilov to some night clubs."

"Assistant Commissar! And we do not come down at Vienna," said Pyotr. "That is an order. Do not imagine that I am unaware of your hopes. It would be easy for you to escape there."

"Would it matter?" asked Nadia. "Why don't we all escape? I have very good friends in Europe who would give Carl and Ugo jobs, and you, Assistant Commissar Danilov ... well, we could set you up in a pig farm."

"A good idea," said Carl, swaying in his seat gently.

" Excellent," said Ugo, putting out a hand to steady him.

"This conversation shall be reported to the appropriate authorities," snapped Pyotr. "Meanwhile, we go on." To emphasize his words he pulled a revolver from his pocket.

"He's incorruptible," said Carl.

"Adamant," said Ugo.

"Pig-headed," said Nadia.

Much later, they were really in trouble. The weather was still bad. Darkness was not far off and, according to Ugo, they were only a short distance from the mountainous frontier of their own country. The petrol was very low. In addition the port engine was giving trouble.

Carl said, "I shall have to look for a place to land."

"Keep on," said Pyotr. "This is a trick."

"Not this time," said Ugo, nodding at the fuel gauge. "Those headwinds have taken it out of us. And listen to that engine."

"Good! Maybe we shall crash," said Nadia. "It is better to die than to go to the salt mines."

"We shan't crash," said Carl hazily. "I am a good pilot and full of good spirits. But I suggest that you all go up into the tail, just in case."

"Keep on," said Pyotr stoutly, waving his revolver.

"Don't be an ass," said Nadia. "If you shoot him we shall crash anyway. Also, when we come down it will be in our own country, so you have nothing to fear."

"It is my pigs I think of. A crash might bring on a premature delivery for Lady Chatterley."

"It is a risk that pig mothers must face if they start flying," said Ugo, and he stood up and led Pyotr towards, the tail. "Carl, you had better SOS our position," he said.

They did crash. Not badly, but enough. Carl brought the machine down through the clouds into a landscape of snow-covered peaks, grey and indigo with the first night shadows. He picked a long valley running down from a high main ridge. He had only enough petrol left for about five minutes' flying, and the faltering port engine made things worse.

But the greatest handicap was the cider laced with whisky which he had taken. There was a long open stretch of snow running down between a fringe of dark pine woods. The trees seemed to dance all over the place.

Back in the tail Ugo cried, "Hold tight!" and he put his arm tightly round Nadia's waist to steady her. Pyotr clutched the side of Lady Chatterley's stall and talked soothingly to her.

They hit the ground, softly at first, bouncing on the smooth snow, and then there was a great splintering crash. Pyotr was jerked forward and his head hit the corner of the packing case. Darkness closed on him like an iron curtain …

When Pyotr came to, he was lying in a large four-poster bed. Sunlight came streaming through a low window which gave him a glimpse of wooden houses and the snowy slopes of a hill dotted with dark pine trees.

Standing at his bedside was a man of about sixty, bluff and brown-faced, and with a thatch of long white hair. He extended an arm and patted Pyotr on the cheek. He wore a leather waistcoat, blue trousers and a yellow shirt, and he had the appearance of an amiable brigand — which in many ways was exactly what Jari Demaru was.

"Welcome, Assistant Commissar Danilov," he boomed. "The whole village welcomes you. We pray to the Holy Mary and her angels and out of the sky she sends help ... Wonderful!"

"What" — said Pyotr a little weakly and realizing that his head was bandaged and aching — "happened?"

Nadia Mariac moved into view. She was dressed in a red skirt, her hair tied back with a ribbon and her arms bare from a loose blouse.

"We crashed. That was yesterday. But Carl managed to send an SOS giving our position first. This is Jan — he keeps this inn."

"And Lady Chatterley?"

"Doing fine!" roared Jan. "A litter of eight, all of them sturdy."

Pyotr began to struggle up. He must go to her at once. But Jan pressed him back. "Don't worry. Tomorrow you can get up, but you're still weak. When you've had some food and wine you'll be better. Until then —"

"But the other pigs," said Pyotr.

"They are being looked after," said Nadia; and she glanced at Jan a little awkwardly.

It was at this moment that Pyotr became aware of a most fragrant odour seeping into the room through the open doorway. Suddenly, as though he had received an electric shock, he jerked upright in bed.

"I can smell roast pork!"

"Of course," Jan soothed him. "Didn't I say you were our saviour? For two months we have been snowed up. This summer our crops failed and our cattle died of a disease. The whole village was starving. The authorities have done nothing about sending us relief. So, we thought —"

"You mean, you've killed one of my pigs!" shouted Pyotr.

"Two," said Nadia. "There are thirty people in the village. One would not be enough."

Pyotr leaped out of bed and then jumped back again. The nightshirt he had been given was absurdly short. He began to shout and storm. The pigs were for breeding purposes. They were not to be eaten. He forbade it ...

It was the beginning of a long argument that carried through intermittently to the next day, when he was well enough to get up and go down to the main room of the inn. There, confronted by Jan and the village elders and Carl, Ugo and Nadia, he had to face facts. There was no food in the village. The people had to eat.

"Which is better, to save the lives of thirty people, or to suffer a little loss to your breeding stock?" asked Jan.

"But the authorities should have sent you food," said Pyotr.

"We are snowed in. It is difficult. Personally, I think they wish us to leave the village and this is their way of doing it."

"Why should they wish you to leave?"

"Because ... Well, we are near the frontier and occasionally we do a little smuggling. You must yourself have enjoyed a contraband cigar —"

"I don't smoke."

"Then a glass of whisky, or given your girl friend a pair of American nylons —"

"I have no girl friend. And no more pigs are to be killed. The authorities have heard our SOS. They will soon dig their way into the valley and bring help."

"Let us hope so," said Jan.

"The pigs are valuable," declared Pyotr. "Help will come, without doubt."

"Maybe," said Nadia. "It is a pity the authorities have not come before this — with food for the villagers. But then they are not pigs."

Pyotr glowered at her. But underneath he was a little disturbed. The authorities should have done something.

He went out to see the pigs and Lady Chatterley. They were all housed in a barn at the back of the inn. Lady Chatterley lay on her side looking very pleased with herself. It was a fine litter.

As he stood there Nadia came up behind him. "They look sweet," she said, leaning over and picking up one of the litter.

"Please," said Pyotr. He took the piglet from her and restored it. "They can easily be injured by improper handling at this stage."

"You are very fond of animals?" asked Nadia.

"It is my work."

"You take it very seriously."

"Life is a very serious business. We have the future to think about."

She was looking at him curiously. "You don't smoke. You don't have a girl friend. You have only the future. You are very good-looking and strong. I think you are kind, too. Will you really let them take me away with the pigs and put me in a salt mine?"

"It is nothing to do with me."

"You know what will happen to me in a salt mine?"

"Please ..."

"You do not like to think of it." She came closer to him. "You find me beautiful?"

"Yes."

"You do not want to kiss me, like Carl and Ugo? Perhaps then you would change your mind about handing me over. You could say I escaped when the plane crashed."

Pyotr frowned. "You are wasting your time."

Nadia smiled. "How can you tell until you have had the kiss?" Suddenly her arms were around his neck and her soft, warm lips on his. After a while Nadia stepped back. "You will change your mind?"

"No," said Pyotr. But he couldn't get any sternness into his face, and his voice was weaker.

Behind them Lady Chatterley suddenly rose and charged her pen bad-temperedly. It was time for her feed.

Two weeks went by and no rescue party came. Pyotr began to feel desperate. As he couldn't stand by and see people starve, ten of his pigs had been eaten. And almost as bad as the pig situation was the Nadia situation. Jan and his villagers were quite prepared to smuggle her over the frontier. But not if Pyotr was going to inform against them.

Nadia herself was still trying to make Pyotr change his mind. Three or four times a day he would turn a corner and find himself in her arms or, as he bent over Lady Chatterley's pen, suddenly feel Nadia's soft lips on the back of his neck.

It was wearing him down. In bed he dreamed about her. Lying awake in the dark he could hear her voice. "You're too nice to give me up. I like you, I really do. Underneath that Party manner you're human. Why don't you escape with me?"

It was a constant barrage. And when she was in his arms, or her lips were on his, it was hard for him to remain resolved in his principles.

Late in the afternoon of the fifteenth day rescue came. A lorry fitted with caterpillar tracks was seen coming up the valley. The whole village assembled outside the inn to welcome it.

Five minutes later Pyotr was closeted with Commissar Androv — his superior at the Ministry of Agriculture — in Jan's little sitting room.

Commissar Androv was a big-jowled, dark shaven man with eyes like Lady Chatterley. He was in a bad temper, too.

"But why have you been so long?" asked Pyotr.

"Because the SOS position was given wrongly. Your pilot is a fool. We've been looking in the wrong valley. And then it took four days to cut through into this one. What about the pigs?"

"They're safe, but —"

Pyotr told him of the villagers' plight. And he finished, "But now you've come with food, they will be all right."

Commissar Androv rose and his face was working with anger. "You're a fool, Danilov! I've brought no food for them. They're a thorn in our side with their independent ways. And if you've let them have the pigs to eat you've not only countenanced the destruction of valuable government property — but you've also interfered with the policy of population redistribution."

"But you can't let people starve."

"In a planned economy, and if policy dictates it, you can," shouted Androv.

Pyotr's lips tightened and his face now had a sternness which no one could ignore. "People are more important than pigs."

"That's treason! You've bungled your mission. Assistant Commissar Danilov, you are under arrest ... And personally I think you'll either be shot or sent to forced labour. And now, where is the girl Nadia Mariac?"

Pyotr stood up. Almost before he knew he was saying it, he heard himself shout: "Arrest me if you like. I've done no wrong. But you can't have her. She escaped back over the frontier following the crash."

"Further bungling! You'll be shot all right ..."

"Go to hell!" snapped Pyotr, and his eyes were blazing.

Pyotr was left in the room. Commissar Androv went out to superintend the loading of the pigs on to the lorry. He was hardly out of the room before Jan entered.

"I was listening," he said. "What are you going to do?"

"Face a trial and rely on the justice of the People's Democracy."

Jan rolled his eyes. "You like to learn the hard way. You'll be shot. Nadia's hiding in the woods. As soon as it's dark she's going over the frontier with Ugo and Carl. You could join them."

"Never! This is my country."

An armed guard came into the room. "Out!" he said to Jan. "This man is under arrest."

From the window, which overlooked the village square, Pyotr watched the lorry being loaded with pigs. The sun was dropping behind the mountains and the pines were throwing long shadows across the snow. Three soldiers, Jan and some villagers — under Commissar Androv's direction — were helping with the loading.

They couldn't shoot him, Pyotr told himself as he watched. He'd done no wrong ... But could he be sure? The government would have let the villagers starve. Policy ... Maybe it would be policy to shoot him.

He saw Lady Chatterley's litter being carried to the lorry, and then came Lady Chatterley, swaying along. They took some time getting her up the ramp into the lorry, but eventually it was done. The guard, watching with Pyotr, said: "All right. Let's go."

Pyotr was marched out of the inn, the guard behind him with his rifle at the ready.

Commissar Androv carne up to him.

"You get up in the cab with me and the lorry driver," Commissar Androv ordered.

As Pyotr moved to the front of the lorry his eye caught Jan's. Jan was standing at the side of the lorry fastening a rope. Maybe it was something in Pyotr's face, or maybe it was just because Jan was so much older and wiser than Pyotr. Anyway, as Pyotr passed, Jan reached inside the lorry and jabbed a long needle into Lady Chatterley's fat flank.

The effect was tremendous.

There was a great, grunting roar of pain from Lady Chatterley. She charged the side of the flimsy stall that had been rigged up at the

81

end of the lorry and crashed through it. Ploughing into the other pigs she carried them before her like a bow wave. The mass of animals thundered against the tailboard of the lorry. The fastenings broke and an avalanche of pigs cascaded to the ground.

A moment later Lady Chatterley and the other pigs were charging across the village square.

The guards and villagers behind the lorry went down before the rush. Commissar Androv leaped round, swearing and shouting to Pyotr's guard to get after the pigs. For two or three moments a squealing, grunting confusion existed in the square while panicking pigs dashed in all directions.

Jan dropped quickly to Pyotr's side. "Run, you fool!" he hissed. "Nadia and the others are up by the crashed plane. I'll see that no one chases you."

Pyotr didn't move.

Run, fool!" urged Jan. "Don't you want to see Nadia again? To be kissed by her? To feel her arms around you? Run!"

Pyotr began to run. Commissar Androv saw him. "Get him!" he bellowed at Jan. "Take some villagers and get him."

"Yes, commissar," said Jan. "But I should point out that if you want to round up these pigs, they were now all heading for the woods down the valley with the guards and villagers after them — you'll need all my people's help."

"Get that man first!" Androv pointed to the small figure of Pyotr racing across the snow towards the head of the valley.

"Yes, commissar. But it may take hours. When darkness comes soon any pig not caught will freeze to death. Pigs are valuable. The country needs them. A man could be shot if he went back to the capital without them, pleading that he thought it better to let them freeze while he went after a traitor. Pigs, not people, are what you have to consider."

Commissar Androv's face gradually inflated. Then he burst out, "Damn you! Pigs then, first."

He and Jan began to lumber down the valley which was noisy with the shouts of the guards and the villagers and the high, frenzied squealing of pigs.

Pyotr went racing across the snow and into the pine trees where the plane had crashed. Nadia, with Ugo, Carl and two guides from the village who were to take them over the frontier, was waiting there.

"You left it almost too late," said Ugo.

"Forward to freedom! " said Carl. But Nadia said nothing. She didn't have to. She just looked at Pyotr and smiled, and Pyotr suddenly put his arms around her and kissed her.

"Break it up," said Ugo.

"Time for that later," said Carl. And they started walking.

STAR STUFF

I suppose my real trouble is that I've never been able to resist a good cash proposition. Sometimes they turn up trumps. But more often not. Not that I mind. Life is full of ups and downs. When you're up you enjoy it and when you're down — well, you have the next up to look forward to.

You know Tania Lamont? Who doesn't? Tania Lamont in *Abruptly, With Love*. Tania Lamont in *Sleeping Wives*. Tania Lamont in *this* and in *that*, and right out there now, across the square, a great neon-lighted cut-out of her in a green sheath dress stretching halfway down the façade of the Paragon and a lot of pigmy faces staring up at her out of the rain. Star worship.

Well, I made her. I gave Tania Lamont her first break. Five years ago. But she was not called Tania Lamont when I first saw her. No, sir. But then a lot of things change when you get into the film business and the first — if you're a girl going places — is usually your name.

At the time I was assistant producer to Otto Heldmaster. It sounds good, doesn't it? The great Heldmaster. But it didn't amount to much. There were three assistant producers and all we did was to sit around waiting to be sent on errands, walk his black poodle, do this, do that — rarely anything of real importance.

Well, one evening he took me to the Savoy for dinner. Not because he liked me particularly, but because he wanted someone to talk to, and I happened to be around. I just sat opposite him and he went on and on about the new picture he had coming up. I didn't say much — Otto liked someone to talk at. It put him off if he were answered.

The great Heldmaster was about fifty, a big fleshy-faced man with a short mat of crisp black hair that looked like astrakhan, and small blue, rather watery eyes that never seemed to blink. He talked about this new film and how some people wanted him to do it in colour and he was damned if he would. People didn't care whether a film was in black and white, colour, or anything so long as it was a good film, and he made good films. Always had. Always would.

And he was damned too if he would take any of the stars they kept pushing at him. The right girl was around somewhere and he would find her and make her. I knew he would, too. He always found what he wanted and it wasn't any good trying to help him.

And then, slap in the middle of his filet mignon, he got up and said goodbye to me, getting my name wrong, and explaining that he must positively be in bed before ten as this was a bad period under his horoscope and he needed the utmost rest for the next three days. He meant it, too. He was a great one for horoscopes and the crystal ball, for never walking under a ladder, for touching wood — he used to carry a little piece of black mahogany in his breast pocket.

So I sat there alone with my thoughts and the prospect of paying the bill and arguing the next day with the accounts people about it because Otto would look blank and not even remember if he had been with me. Anyway, I finished my steak and passed on to coffee and with it the waiter brought a note asking me to join another table for liqueurs. He pointed out the table across the room. It had only one occupant, a dark-haired woman in a white dress with a sparkle about her neck and hands that looked expensive even at that distance.

I went over. When opportunity knocks, you always want to answer. She was in her early twenties, and even without the diamonds she could knock your eye out.

She said, "I saw Mr. Heldmaster leave you. I hope you didn't resent my note,"

"I'm here," I said. "Anyway, I've a feeling you're more interested in Mr. Heldmaster than in me. But I warn you, though I'm perfectly willing to get you an interview with him, it won't work. I've tried it before, for money and for love. He just likes to find his stars for himself."

"I'm aware of that, Mr. —?"

"Speedwell, Jimmy."

The waiter hovered and, after she had said Cointreau, I said Grand Marnier and then I went on, to her, "I'm sorry — I can't help."

"I'm sure you can." She smiled at me and it was a good smile. She had everything, including money and I couldn't think why she wanted more. But some women are like that.

"How?" I asked.

85

"I want to be a film star. It sounds terrible said like that, doesn't it? But I do. And I'll be frank. I don't want to do years of dreary repertory work and so on for it. I want to go in at the top."

"Who wouldn't?"

But she gave me that smile again and there was a lot of calculation behind it. "It can be done. You know Mr. Heldmaster. From what I hear he always goes on hunches. Now, you find a way for him to discover me and I'll pay you two thousand pounds the day he signs me to a contract. A hundred now, as a guarantee of good faith — and the understanding between us that our little arrangement remains a dead secret forever."

"With all due respect," I said, "I think you're crazy. I don't have any way of doing it."

She stood up. "You look to me like the kind of young man who can find a way. My name is Nicholson — Miss — and my telephone number is in this envelope with the hundred pounds." She dropped an envelope before me.

"You came here with this envelope all prepared?"

"I've got a good intelligence service. Mr. Heldmaster frequently dines here with one of his assistant producers."

She left, trailing a clutch of mink from one hand and without looking back.

I slept on it for three nights. £2000. I was fed up with being an assistant producer. With £2000 I could take off for the South of France for six months and do that thing I really like doing — which is not having to work. And then when I thought that there was no possible way, Otto handed it to on a platter.

He pushed his head round office door and called to me one afternoon, "Harry!"

"Jimmy, Mr. Heldmaster."

"Oh, yes, Jimmy. Ring Mrs. Zaremba and tell her I'd like to change my weekly appointment from Wednesday to Thursday the same time."

"Yes, sir."

But I didn't ring her. I went round to her flat in Chelsea. Zaremba, I was sure, wouldn't be offended at the prospect of £200. That kind of money doesn't float out of crystal balls when you tickle them.

I put it to her straight. She was a granite-chinned woman with a pair of eyes like black marbles and a gipsy scarf over her head — the kind I was sure, who didn't want any finessing about money.

I talked and she listened and occasionally she nodded, and there the table between us was her crystal ball with a velvet cloth over it.

When I'd finished she said, "You are in love with this girl, aren't you?"

"I am." She would have to do better with her crystal ball than that to get my personal trade. "Will you do it? Please." I even got a catch in my voice for her.

She nodded. "I will. Two hundred and fifty pounds. Fifty now. Two hundred more if it comes off."

Well, it was fifty more than I'd bargained for, but I agreed and went straight out and telephoned Miss Nicholson. There was no need to beat about the bush.

I said, "You know Mr. Heldmaster has a suite on the third floor of the Royal Curzon Hotel?"

"Yes."

"Well, by hook or by crook, and by this coming Thursday, I want you to take a suite on the floor below. Any suite on the second floor will do. But they all have different coloured entrance doors — blue, yellow, green, red, and so on. When you've got a suite just let me know the colour of the door, Can you do that?"

"If I have to buy the hotel."

"Good. Now, the next step. On Thursday you stay in that suite all afternoon — until midnight if necessary. Don't have a maid or anyone else in. Whoever knocks on the door, you answer it in person. Some time after four Mr. Heldmaster'll knock. Just pretend you don't know him. React how you like. But he won't take anything from you except your signature on a contract. He'll discover you. Okay?"

"You're sure this is going to work?"

"It can't fail. It's a crystal-ball certainty."

It would be, too. Otto could be as keen as a hawk, but the fortune-telling stuff put blinkers on him, He'd held up production on his last film for two weeks because some star or planet was in the wrong house or quarter or something.

87

Well, I bit my nails until Otto went off for his appointment on Thursday. I'd got the message from Miss Nicholson that her door was a green one and had passed the information to Mrs. Zaremba.

I sat there imagining the interview. It wasn't hard — I'd done the script for it. I could hear her voice as she hung over the crystal ball and Otto lapped it all up ... "Yes, something comes, the shadows draw back. I see you, Mr. Heldmaster, walking, walking through the streets, walking up to a hotel entrance and all about you there is a green aura — of thought, of worry, and I feel that you are waiting for guidance.

"Oh, how strong your vibrations are, glowing so green ... You go through the lobby like a man in a dream, a green haze about you, you walk to the marble stairway — it's a lovely stairway with carved fish, big fish, at the bottom. You walk up to the second floor and you turn right and the doors of the suites stretch out before you.

"I can't see the numbers on them — but they are all different colours. But like a man in a dream, compelled by your own destiny, you go straight to the green door and you knock ...

"Oh, dear, it begins to fade ... No, no, I see the door open and a young, dark-haired, beautiful woman stands there — a stranger to you — and on your face I see a sudden blaze of revelation. This girl is the answer — the answer to your problem. Oh, it's going fast. The crystal ball is getting clouded ..."

The marble stairway in Otto's hotel, the Royal Curzon, had two carved dolphins at the foot. It couldn't miss.

And that is how Otto found the girl for his next film. At five o'clock I got a call from an excited Otto to bring a cameraman over to his suite. We went over there. Otto's man let us in. In the lounge was Otto, and a dark-haired girl stood by the fireplace with her back to us.

Otto said, "This, gentlemen, is the young lady who is going to star in my next film. Under the influence of the stars, guided and inspired by my own aura as though in a soft green haze, I have been led to her."

The girl turned. She was dark-haired and lovely. But it wasn't Miss Nicholson.

Otto introduced her to us. "Miss Janet Bolton," he said. "But we'll change that. Just think, I found her in this hotel! — on the floor below where she worked as a secretary to an old lady who has a suite there."

Well, there it was. Less than a year later Janet Bolton was Tania Lamont.

As soon as I could get away rang Miss Nicholson. It was a brief interview. No one had knocked on her door.

I said, "What the hell happened then? He was still mumbling about his green aura when I left him. He must have knocked on your door."

"Nobody knocked, I tell you. That fool Mrs. Zaremba must have got it wrong."

"No, I've already checked with her. Green, she said. Green. And Otto's babbling green, too."

I could hear her breathing angrily over the telephone, then she snapped, "That damned fool Otto Heldmaster must be colour blind."

Although she didn't know it — and I didn't find out until an intimate friend of Otto's let it slip one night when he'd had too many brandies — Miss Nicholson was dead right. Otto had been colour blind all his life. That's why he'd never make colour films.

Green and red looked just the same to him. He'd simply knocked on the wrong door — a red one I checked later, and got the right girl — for there was no doubt about the girl. Tania Lamont had star stuff in her all the time — just take a look across the square in front of the Paragon.

SHE KNEW WHAT SHE WANTED

Going up in the lift to his flat, Freddie Marburg went over in his mind all the things that had gone wrong that day. Everything at the rehearsal of his new play had gone wrong. Lottie Wainwright, who had the leading part, was no good, and he knew that he was going to have to get rid of her. That would mean fireworks. Also, her long speech in the first act was no good, and he had spent most of the morning rewriting it on stage and still wasn't sure of it.

The stage designer didn't seem to have a clue what he wanted for the third act set. In addition, his *sole meunière* at lunch had been like a piece of old india rubber — and he had lost the key to his flat. This last mishap was his own fault because he had a habit, when annoyed, of swinging his bunch of keys round on the end of its chain.

To top it all, in a weak moment, he had agreed to have his French agent, who was in town, come round that evening and discuss details of a Paris production. The man spoke hardly any English, and Freddie felt too worn out to make the effort speaking French. He just wanted to put his feet up and relax — relax and forget that there were such things as plays and films and Marburg Productions.

He walked along to his flat door and rang the bell. The lost key meant nothing. His man, Ankers, would let him in. Only, Ankers didn't let him in.

The door was opened by a girl. Now Freddie, a young man himself, was used to taking the measure of most young women pretty quickly — and of pretty ones a little quicker than quickly, because usually there was only one thing they wanted from him: a chance to make good, a part in a play, the helping hand on the road to stardom.

He groaned quietly to himself as he ran his eyes over this one. Some girls would do anything to draw his attention to themselves, he thought.

This one was about twenty-two, good figure, pretty but not dumb-looking. She was blonde and she wore a simple green silk dress that was in very good taste.

Freddie approved the dress, but not the automatic in her right hand with which she casually beckoned him into his own home!

Wearily, keeping his irritability for later, Freddie said: "Okay. Another stunt girl crazy for a contract from Marburg Productions. What part do you fancy?"

The girl smiled, motioned him towards the lounge and spoke to him in a pleasant voice, but what she said was "Go in and put your feet up. You've had a bad day. What you need is a drink."

Freddie did not quarrel with this. He went into the lounge, flopped into an armchair and kicked off his shoes with a sigh.

Then he said: "Where's Ankers, by the way? Shot?"

The girl, now by the sideboard and reaching for a bottle, the automatic lying handy on the polished top, said "No. I phoned him a couple of hours ago, Mr. Marburg, with a message from you that he could take the evening off. Also —" she reached for a glass "— I took the liberty of phoning your French agent and told him that, regretfully, you had to cancel your invitation to him to come here this evening but that you would be getting in touch with him during the next few days."

"Well, that's one mark in your favour. You speak French?"

She nodded. "And German and Spanish."

Freddie lit a cigarette. "Well, get on with it," he said. "They usually start tearing into some part they've rehearsed. I've had three Juliets, a Desdemona and a St. Joan in the last six months. None of them was any good. You girls —" he sighed deeply "— what you'll do to get on the stage! And why the gun, anyway? You haven't explained."

Busy mixing a drink, the girl said "Because when you do give me a contract, I know you'll love to have a good story to tell your friends. Girl with gun in your flat, holding you up, forcing you to listen and then making good."

"You've got a point there," said Freddie. "If you make good. You seem to know a lot about me. What's your name? I'll need to know for the contract."

"Elsie Brown."

"As a name, it stinks."

91

"I don't mean to change it."

She handed him the drink and stepped back, watching him, smiling all the time, the automatic steady in her right hand.

Freddie sipped at the drink and his eyes opened wide. It was exactly as he liked it. He nodded at the glass. "How did you know about this?" he enquired.

Elsie picked up his shoes, walked through into his bedroom, and came back with his slippers and put them in front of him.

"The barman at the theatre," she said. "And Ankers. 'Mr. Marburg always drinks negroni — equal parts Campari, gin and Italian vermouth, ice, lemon and a flick of soda.' By the way — here's your door key" She dropped a key into his lap.

"Where the devil did you get that?"

"It flew off your key ring while you were taking rehearsals at the theatre this morning."

"You were at the theatre?"

"I've been there every morning for the last week — tucked away at the back of the stalls. You wouldn't have noticed."

"But how did you get in? I've got a strict rule about strangers."

"I phoned the stage doorkeeper at the beginning of the week, said I was your secretary and that you had given instructions for him to admit a Miss Elsie Brown."

Freddie took another sip of his drink. It was delicious and did something to his nerves. "All right," he said, "let's have your piece and get it over. "

Elsie walked to a chair and lifted a large handbag. She pulled out a silver cigarette case and walked over to him with it.

"By the way, here's the case you lost two days ago. It was under a seat in the dress circle. You went up there to get a better view of the third act set. If you will put your feet up on the back of seats, you must expect things to fall from your pocket from time to time.

Freddie, for the first time, smiled. "You're quite a girl, aren't you? Right on the ball. But that doesn't mean you can act, I'm afraid. However, for this drink, at least you deserve an audition. What have you got in mind? How about Rosalind for a change? I haven't had a Rosalind for weeks."

Elsie drew a slim folder from her handbag and handed it to Freddie. "This is the big speech in the first act. I thought you'd like to hear what it sounds like with the alterations you made this morning."

Freddie stared at the folder and then opened it. There were two or three pages of neatly typed script inside it.

"But I only made these alterations this morning!"

"I know, Mr. Marburg. But at the moment I am a shorthand-typist and as you've guessed, I want to be more than that. I took down your alterations when you went through them with Miss Wainwright, and then I retyped the scene."

"You don't miss any tricks, do you?"

"I'm very ambitious and know what I want. Is that wrong?"

"No. Not at all. In fact, it's refreshing. Most of the Juliets and St. Joans rely chiefly on off-the-shoulder dresses, or lots of leg and a come-hither look to make up for their histrionic lapses. Not that there's anything wrong with your general assembly lines … But can you act?"

"I don't know."

"Modest as well?" Freddie chuckled, but without much humour. "Well, let's hear you. Do you want the script?"

"No. I know it by heart."

"That's more than most."

Freddie lay back, closed his eyes and listened lazily as Elsie went right through the speech she had prepared. When she had finished he looked at her, his face showing nothing. He held up his empty glass. "Another, and this time —"

"I know," she said, taking the glass. "After the first, only half the amount of gin and no soda." She went to the sideboard and began to make the drink.

"You know," said Freddie as she brought the drink back, "you really are an unusual girl. You can act. You're good. You gave those alterations just what I wanted. No, no —" he held up his hand as she made to speak "— just let me think." He sipped his drink and was silent for a while. He seemed to concentrate absorbedly on the stem of his glass.

Then he said: "All right — I maybe mad — but I'll take a chance on you. Lottie's going. She doesn't know it yet, but she is. That I can promise you. Think you could handle the part? "

For a moment Elsie looked down at him in surprise. Then she said: "Mr. Marburg, a life on the stage is the most insecure and

93

unsatisfying that I could imagine. I want to travel. I speak three languages. I want to be indispensable to someone. Surely I've shown you that I'm capable of all these things. I want to be your personal secretary."

Freddie stared at her amazed. "But I've got a personal secretary," he said, "the best in the world. She's on holiday at the moment but she'll be back next week."

Elsie Brown shook her head. "No, Mr. Marburg. When your secretary returns from her holiday, she's going to tell you that she's married and leaving you. She's been secretly engaged to my present boss for three months, and they were married four days ago. Am I hired?"

He grinned, this time more warmly. "I haven't the slightest doubt that you've got the letter of agreement from me already typed in your handbag."

"Of course, Mr. Marburg." Elsie fished in her bag. "And here's your pen to sign it. You left it in the theatre bar yesterday when making sketches of the way you wanted the third act set to be altered." Elsie handed him the pen and the letter of agreement.

Freddie signed and, as he did so, he said drily: "Seems to me there's only one way to keep a good personal secretary these days — marry her." He looked up.

Elsie Brown just smiled.

DEATH WORE GREEN

There are some people, kind, honest and good-hearted, who seem to have no luck in life at all. Joe Barker was like that. He was a decent, unassuming Londoner of twenty-five with sandy hair, blue eyes, a square pleasant mouth and a firm conviction that nothing would ever go right for him.

No matter how hard he tried, he never seemed to keep a job long; and no matter how nice and polite he was to them he never seemed to keep a girl long. This last worried him because at heart he was longing to be a family man and to have a home of his own. One way and another he was always getting into trouble, or doing or saying the wrong thing. In the end he got quite used to it and was no longer surprised at his misfortunes.

It was no surprise to him, therefore, when he fell overboard from the *S.S. Baroda*, five days out of Manila, somewhere in the Pacific Ocean.

Joe had gotten a job aboard as a cook. Clearing up his galley late one night, he came on deck with a can of garbage, walked aft to the stern where a section of the guard rail had been taken out and pitched the rubbish overboard. It was a fine night, ablaze with stars, and Joe put the can down and lit a cigarette. Then, as he turned to bend down and pick up the can and go back to his galley, his foot slipped on some potato peelings that had spilled on the deck. The next minute he was overboard — as clean as a whistle and with no time to shout, and the splash he made was lost in the streaming wake from the *S.S. Baroda*'s screws.

By the time he came to the surface, cleared his mouth of salt water and began to shout, his ship was two hundred yards ahead and not a soul heard him. Joe trod water and watched the lights of his ship fade away into the darkness. He knew that it would be early the next morning before he was missed and, knowing what his luck was like, he guessed that they would never find him.

He was wearing a shirt and drill trousers and was barefooted. The only thing of value he had on him was a waterproof wrist watch which he had bought in Manila and of which he was very proud. He kept looking at the luminous dial of this to see how the time was going, and it seemed to go very slowly indeed. Long before dawn came, Joe knew that he was getting very tired and couldn't last much longer. He made gentle little movements of his hands to keep himself afloat and he thought of the wife and kids he would now never have, of the little business he would now never start, and he tried to figure out just who would really miss him and couldn't think of a soul.

Some time toward dawn he began to go a bit fuzzy in the head and kept imagining he could hear noises, voices calling and sounds of boats passing, but even in his exhausted state he had enough sense to know that it was only his fancy. Just as the sun edged above the far horizon and spread the sea with a silver and gold sparkle of light, Joe lost consciousness.

When he came round he felt for a moment that the whole thing had been a dream which was still going on. He was lying on his back on a beach and feeling very ill. The sun, high in the sky now, was baking his clothes dry. Over his head palm trees tossed their spear leaves in a gentle wind, and distantly he could hear the noise of waves breaking over some reef.

Crowding around him were six native girls. They were jabbering away among themselves, highly excited, and sometimes touching him as though they weren't really convinced that he existed. As for Joe, he was considerably embarrassed. The girls were as beautiful a bunch as he had seen in his life, but their idea of dress seemed to be a grass skirt and a few hibiscus flowers stuck in their hair.

Joe blushed and shut his eyes. He felt himself propped up by a soft arm, and a drinking shell was pressed against his lips. He opened his eyes and drank, and the girls nodded and clapped their hands approvingly. The one who was propping him up had a much lighter skin than the others. She smiled at him, wrinkled her pretty nose, and he saw that her eyes were brown with flecks of gold in them. Joe smiled back and kept his eyes strictly on her face. It seemed the polite thing to do and saved him embarrassment.

However, Joe's embarrassment was something he had to learn to live with. After a time four native men appeared carrying a litter with a canopy of palm leaves, and Joe was loaded aboard and borne in style from the beach to a small village. He was put in a hut, given food and coconut wine; and because the wine was strong he fell asleep, hoping that when he woke again the whole thing would not turn out to be a dream.

It didn't; and by the next day Joe knew where he was and what it was all about. He had been pulled out of the sea by the six girls who had been out fishing in a canoe, and he was on a small atoll named Alifa which was one of the Caroline Islands and well off any trade routes. Not for twenty years had a white man been to the island. But that wasn't the reason why Joe was such a sensation. The explanation was given to him by an old man called Raua who had once been a mission boy in New Guinea and spoke some English.

"On Alifa," he said, "always plenty more women than men. Six girls who rescue you have no young men to marry. All want be bride to you."

"What? All six?" Joe's eyes widened.

"No, no. We good people. One man, one wife. You marry one girl from six. New blood, new babies, maybe plenty boy babies. Not like last time. Gods send white stranger from the sea. He pick bride of gods, but only have damn girl babies so, women put him in boat and send him away ... Maybe drowned, Perhaps sharks eat."

"You really mean I'm expected to marry one of these six girls?" Joe couldn't get over it.

"Damn sure."

Joe, for the first time in his life, felt that his luck was turning. Usually girls wouldn't look at him. Now he had six to choose from. At this moment Joe's eye fell on Lei-lei who came up to the but with his midday drink of coconut wine. She was the lighter skinned girl whom he had first noticed on the beach, and much more since.

Although all the young girls looked after him and treated him like a king, Lei-lei went out of her way more than the others to see he had everything. There was no doubt about it that she had taken a fancy to him; and, if the truth had to be known, Joe had taken a fancy to her.

"Well," said Joe, "it won't be difficult to pick the girl I want."

Raua shook his head. "Very difficult to pick. Six girls all want you. No can agree which have you. So, young girls go up to mountain top and dance for gods. Then gods say which one will be bride. Always same thing when more than one girl want same man."

"Doesn't the man get any say in this?" asked Joe indignantly.

"Damn sure, no. Women run things on Alifa. After gods pick bride, young girls come down and dance for you. You pick right one, if not ..."

"If not, what?"

"Everyone take spears and kill you, or gods get angry,"

"What?" Joe frowned. "But how am I expected to know which one to pick?" Rata's wrinkled old face split with a sly grin. "You pay Raua well. He tell you when time come how to pick bride of gods. Women no want young man killed. They make plan with Raua. Give sign. Very easy."

"But I've got no money. How can I pay you?"

Raua chuckled. "Fine watch you wear. You make present to Raua? Damn sure, yes?"

Joe handed over his watch.

There were two weeks to go before the new moon and the bride-picking ceremony. In those days Joe and Lei-lei saw a lot of each other. They went for walks together and Joe taught her a little English, and she told him that she was the daughter of the last white visitor, a Scots engineer who had fallen overboard drunk from his ship. In no time at all Joe had lost his heart to her, and Lei-lei felt the same way about Joe. On the night before the new moon they walked on the beach together, and Joe slipped his arm around her waist.

"If you're not elected, lass," said Joe, "I don't know what I'll do. No, that's not honest. No man wants his back full of spears. Oh, damn!"

Lei-lei looked up at him tenderly, "Lei-lei love Joe. Joe love Lei-lei, Gods maybe pick Lei-lei for bride,"

"Not if I know my luck ..." sighed Joe.

At noon the next day them was a ceremonial feast, suckling pig, fish, taros, bananas, breadfruit and plenty of coconut wine. Afterward the six young girls, singing and dancing, filed away into the jungle toward the mountain that dominated the little island. Joe waited under a palm tree, and the rest of the village sat around polishing and sharpening their spears, full of good humor for they were sure that Raua would tip the young white man off which girl to pick.

As dusk began to fall, the sound of singing was heard from the jungle, and then into the village clearing came the procession of young girls, all carrying torches. Joe, sitting on a dais in the center of

98

the clearing with Raua beside him, said, "Come on, Raua — how do I tell?" He was overanxious, angry and a little tipsy from too much coconut wine. Fine thing that a man couldn't choose his own wife!

Raua said, "Very easy. Raua, he arrange sign. All girls wear grass skirts, each different color, green, yellow, so on — but bride of gods wear red skirt." And with that Raua slipped away.

Joe sat there with Raua's words ringing in his head. Pick the girl with the red skirt. But how could he?

"Hey, Raua!" he shouted for the old man, but Rana was lost among the dancers. Wasn't it just like his luck, thought Joe, his heart sinking as he saw the villagers, spears in hand, watching him. For any other man to pick out the one girl among the six in a red skirt would have been easy. But not for Joe. One of the things that had always embarrassed him, could even have been the reason for a certain inferiority complex in him, was the fact that he was colour blind and couldn't tell red from green. All reds looked green to him.

The young girls swirled round him, clapping their hands and swaying, all of them wearing grass skirts and garlands of flowers. Wilder and wilder grew the dance, and then suddenly with a great shout they stopped and stood silently before him. Joe rose, his eyes sweeping along the row. There was a cold sweat on his brow. For the life of him he couldn't tell which was wearing the red skirt. Out of the six girls he eliminated four, but both the last two seemed to him to be wearing green. And Lei-lei was one of the two. But did she have the red skirt or the other? Then, because he loved Lei-lei. Joe stepped down, said a silent prayer to himself that he might be right, and took her by the hand,

The next moment, from the howl of rage that went up from all the other women and the sudden flash of spear tips in the torchlight, he knew that he had chosen wrong.

Lei-lei saved him. She turned and ran for the jungle, dragging Joe with her. Joe never understood how they made it, but they did. Lei-lei went like the wind and he followed. Half an hour later the sound of pursuit was far behind them and, when they reached the other side of the island, Lei-lei Found a fishing canoe and they pushed off into the darkness. Two days later a liner picked them up.

They keep a little restaurant now, and a more devoted couple it would be hard to find. They've got two boys and a girl, and when the kids are in bed at night Lily Barker looks across at her Joe thinking what a wonderful man he is. The bravest in the world … the kind of man who for love of her defied the island gods and risked death from her peoples' spears.

And Joe, for his part, has become expert at hiding his colour blindness. Although he loves her with all his heart, he has had the good sense not to tell her the truth behind his choice. After all, in the happiest marriage, there's no harm in keeping some things to yourself.

TROUBLE IN THE CITY

Baruch looked down at his wife and she smiled back at him. She was young still and so was he, and he was thinking of the days of their courtship, of the evenings when he would wait beneath the olives on the outskirts of the village and she would come as the sun was setting to sit on the well wall with him — tall and beautiful, the wings of her dark hair escaping from under her headscarf, her dark eyes bright with love, and her body swaying like a young sapling. Her smile now was brave, but he knew that behind it lay pain. The thought made him stir with impotent anger, a fear which was less for herself than for the child she carried, their first child.

She said, "What did the doctor say?"

He reached down and took her thin hand into his own hard brown workman's fingers. "That the child is well within you. There is no need to worry. Your sickness is one which can be cured with these new drugs."

"New drugs? But they will cost money."

"I can find it." He was thinking of the doctor, a man who allowed himself no pity when he treated the poor for fear of being swamped by it; a hard, competent professional man who had bluntly said, "Unless she has these drugs she will die when the child comes. Though the child may live."

"Where will you find the money?" she asked.

He smiled and stretched out his hands. "A man can work." But when he had left her and gone down to the one room which lay below the bedroom, he stood rubbing his eyes, wondering how he should begin. A man could work — but it would take a year's work to buy these drugs. And the doctor would give him no credit. His wife had to have these drugs now, within the next few days.

For a moment he had a picture of himself alone, his wife gone- the blackness of the thought made his face tighten with anger. Work could not help him because he had no time. He must go to Adan who lived on the outskirts of the city. But it was no good going to Adan with empty hands. Adan was a good man, but he, too, was like the

101

doctor, without pity, because in a country so poor and so disturbed with riots pity solved nothing if a man wished to stay alive.

Baruch looked round the room. He had to sell whatever he had of value. And there was very little. They lived on the edge of starvation and their possessions were few. He went round the room collecting those things which he thought might fetch money with Adan: two worn silver spoons which his wife had brought with her on her marriage, a carved wooden box with an ebony top, a silk sheet worked in tiny threads of purple and gold which had been a wedding present, and from the floor near the door the large dyer's bowl in which they kept the kindling twigs for starting their fire. The bowl had been his father's — a dyer — and he could remember as a boy watching his father dipping the lengths of cloth into it, raising and lowering them, and the dye dripping-red, green, and yellow-on his arms.

He put the pathetic collection on the rough table and wrapped them in an old shirt of his own, and he knew that by themselves they were not enough. These new drugs were expensive.

He picked up the bundle and went out. There was only one thing to do, and it was the kind of thing which was always happening to people like himself. You worked hard and planned to make life a little easier, but somehow you never got a chance to catch up with yourself.

Most of the week he was away, peddling cheap goods in the mountain villages, his wares loaded on the back of his donkey. Twice the donkey had foaled and the colt had died. But the third time the colt had lived. With two beasts of burden he could increase his trade, make life a little easier. And now, when he had an almost full-grown colt and looked forward to travelling in the mountains, carrying twice as much to sell, able to increase his business, he would have to sell the colt to Adan. But it had to be done.

With these few household pieces and the colt, Adan would give him enough money to buy the drugs which his wife needed.

He went out from the gloom of the house. The fierce sunlight slashed his eyes and a dry wind whipped up the dust into his face. He went across the sun-bitten square to the stables behind the inn where he kept his donkey in return for work he did for the innkeeper. People greeted him as he crossed the square, and he acknowledged them absentmindedly. He was well liked and normally would stop and chat, but now his thoughts were full of his wife.

He went round behind the inn to the small enclosure where the donkey and the colt were kept. The innkeeper's boy was sitting on the top rail of the fence, whittling at a stick with his knife. He nodded to Baruch and jumped down.

From the centre of the enclosure the old pack donkey looked up and, seeing Baruch, came slowly across and thrust its muzzle into his caressing hand. But Baruch was scarcely aware of the animal's actions. There was no sign of the colt in the enclosure.

"Where's the colt?" he asked the boy. "But you sent for it, master."

"What?" Baruch caught the boy by the shoulder and drew him close.

"You sent for it. About two hours ago. Two men came and asked for it."

"What men, and what did they say?" Panic struck at Baruch. In a poor country nothing was safe, and if his colt had gone ...

"I didn't know them. But they said, 'The Master needs the colt.' So I let them take it, and they went away towards the city —"

But Baruch was no longer with the boy. He had turned and with his bundle over his shoulder was striding back to the square, heading for the road to the city. Anger and panic misted his brain. The boy had been tricked. The country was full of rogues.

He had to get quickly to the city if he wished to see his colt again. It would be taken into the market, sold, and be out of the place within a few hours. But nobody was going to steal his colt. He could recognise it anywhere. Let him just catch a glimpse of it.

He half ran, half walked, jog-trotting down the dusty length of road, the sweat pouring off him, and he had always in his mind the picture of his wife lying in the hot bedroom, her body wasting and yet growing with child-his wife who had come each evening through the purpling dusk to the well where they would talk, and plan their life together, his wife, the great pearl of his life ...

There were quite a few people on the road and some of them called to him, but he hurried past, a man obsessed. He didn't often go to the city, only when he needed to see Adan and stock up with fresh wares. There was always trouble in the city, political riots, and the soldiers smashing through the angry crowds, clearing the streets.

A poor man with a living to make kept away from that kind of thing. Often there were demonstrations, speeches, appeals, and always trouble. Usually he did not go into the centre of the city, for Adan's house was on the outskirts. But now he pressed on, passing Adan's house, for he had thought for only one thing, to get to the market quickly. A thief would take the colt there right away.

When he reached the city centre he was covered with dust, and his body was so wet with sweat that his clothes clung to him, and his mouth was parched with thirst. In the narrow streets he had to slow his pace to that of the crowds. Something was afoot again today, the crowd surging forward, shouting and waving their arms, but he let the noise and confusion sweep over him, uncomprehending because his mind held only the thought of his colt. Then as he neared the market which was close to the temple, he was caught up in a great crowd, close-packed so that he could scarcely make any progress.

And then suddenly he saw his colt. Baruch was a tall man, and over the heads of the crowd he could see a small procession passing towards the temple, and at the head of the procession was a man riding his colt! He recognised it at once, and even in the moment of recognition he felt surprise, for the colt was unbroken, had never had a weight on its back before, and yet here it ambled in the stir of the noisy crowd carrying its rider without so much as a buck or a kicking up of its heels!

The next moment Baruch was struggling towards the colt, fighting his way through the packed crowd and shouting, "Stop him! Stop, thief! That's my colt!"

But he might as well have shouted against a gale of wind. Nobody heard him, nobody heeded him, and the crowd made a wall against which he struggled in vain. Just for one brief second Baruch thought that the man on the colt must have heard him, for he turned his head and looked across the crowd towards him, and again Baruch had a moment of surprise for it was a friendly, calm face, an honest face — and yet the man rode his colt.

All he could do now was to try to follow, to go with the crowd, but as they neared the temple he lost sight of the head of the procession and was forced aside and then jammed into the angle of a house wall where the crowd, coming to a halt, held him. All he could see was the heads of his neighbours and all he could hear was the roar of voices and he could not tell whether the voices were angry or joyful.

Something was happening up there by the temple but he could see nothing and he could think only of his colt and his wife and the drugs; despair made him sob with frustration as he struggled to fight his way from the wall angle.

And then the soldiers came, clearing the streets as he had seen them do a hundred times before. No pity, no gentleness, just sweeping down on the crowd in an armoured, unbreakable line, and the crowd surged, turned, and broke, streaming away before the soldiers.

When Baruch turned and tried to go with them, to escape the indiscriminate striking and violence of the oncoming soldiers, he tripped and fell and the crowd went over him and his hand lost its grip on his bundle of household possessions. Feet smashed against him and he lay on the ground, feeling his body pounded by the passage of the panic-stung crowd.

And then the crowd passed and he saw his bundle lying close to him.   He grabbed at it and began to rise to his knees. But he got no farther. The soldiers were on him, spread wide across the street, flaying everything in front of them. A sergeant bore down on him, shouting and swearing, and he saw the man's hand rise high, saw the flash of steel in the hard sunlight. Instinctively Baruch threw up his hands to protect his head and he felt the great shock of the blow strike against the metal bowl inside his bundle.

When he came to, he was in Adan's house. The bearded merchant was sitting behind his table and Baruch was lying on a couch, while one of Adan's men held a drinking cup to his lips.

Adan said, "After the riot one of my men found you, recognised you, and brought you here, Baruch. What were you doing in the centre of the city?"

Baruch struggled to a sitting position. His head cleared slowly.

On the table in front of Adan he saw his few household possessions miserably laid out. Suddenly the memory of the colt and his wife surged bitterly back into his mind.

"My wife is ill, Adan. She must have expensive new drugs to save her, to make her well for the coming of our child. Those things in front of you I would have sold to you for the money. But I knew they would not be enough. My new colt also I would have brought to you, but it was stolen and I came to the city to look for it. Now it is too late ..."

Adan nodded gravely. He knew Baruch. He knew what must be in his mind. Slowly he reached out and took the old dyeing bowl into his hands. There was a great gash across it where the soldier's sword had struck it. The metal, stained with so many colours; almost black with years of use, was dented and knocked badly out of shape.

"This bowl," said Adan, "was your father's?"

"Yes, Adan. My father's and his father's before him, and before that it was in our family when all the men were soldiers. It came, I believe, from Egypt."

"It did indeed," said Adan. "And you have no need to worry about your colt. Whoever took it did you a great service. Look, see where the sword struck it —" he handed the bowl to Baruch.

The great gash shone brightly.

"This," said Adan, "is no ordinary metal dyeing bowl. It is gold, pure gold — looted, maybe, by one of your soldier ancestors from Egypt. Give praise, Baruch, that your colt was taken and so you came into the city centre, for this bowl will save your wife and child and make you a rich man."

Baruch looked down at the bowl in his hands, and suddenly his heart was light and full of gladness, and he could see his wife, dark and beautiful, sitting under the olive tree behind his house, holding in her arms their first child.

THE LION TAMER

It was really the coloured poster on the side of the Rose and Crown which started it all. Freddie had never seen anything half so beautiful in all his life; nor any man so strong and magnificent as the resplendent Herculax. He had read, with some hesitation but more application than ever characterised his reading at the village school, the words under the poster:

HERCULAX THE LION-TAMER!
HERCULAX THE MIGHTY!
THE UNCROWNED KING OF THE BEASTS!
PERFORMING TROUPE OF LIONS,
LEOPARDS AND TIGERS!

In smaller type the public was invited not to miss this circus sensation, not to let slip this opportunity of experiencing the greatest thrill that any circus could give. Freddie did not need the captions to tell him that Herculax's display with animals was stupendous, hair-raising, a unique spectacle. He could see from the poster that it was.

As he climbed across the broken turf of the valley side towards the woods that ran along the ridge, he carried with him a vivid picture of the poster. There was Herculax, dressed only in a leopard skin, with heavy gold bangles around his wrists and ankle, his long hair starting from his head like a black wave and coiling it, the air from his hand the vicious thong of the leather whip with which he controlled his animals.

And the animals … lions, leopards, tigers, they were all there; some perched on tall stools, some forming groups and bridges with the aid of wooden blocks, one tiger leaping through a paper hoop which Herculax held aloft, and a leopard. with a wicked snarl wrinkling its features, balancing on a red-and-white ball.

All the animals seemed to acknowledge the mastery of that dominant, central figure. There he stood, the mighty Herculax, proudly, firmly, commandingly, and Freddie's little face tightened as he thought of his swelling muscle, those brown arms and the fearles look that Herculax gave the animals from above his long, waxed moustache

He was so occupied with his thoughts that he walked into a small gorse bush and fell. He picked himself up, retrieved the wicker basket which had trundled from his hand, and went on. He had not sensed the pricks of the gorse, although his small knee showed a few faint red lines of blood.

Ninepence, he supposed, was an awful lot of money. When he thought about it, he knew it was, although at first, after his mother had told him that she could not let him have it to visit the circus he had thought her very mean. He had tried to explain that it wasn't the circus so much, not the elephants and the performing seals, or even the wire-walkers, but Herculax that he wanted to see … She didn't understand and he could not make himself clear.

He had wished for a moment that he had possessed some of Herculax's power. Then he would have looked fixedly at his mother and said: "I must have ninepence!" and she would have given it to him obediently. He had tried to do that later in the evening when his father returned from the farm. He had looked at him hard and said: "I must have ninepence!"

His father had glanced up from his meal, laughed not unkindly, and replied: "Then you'll have to earn it!" Freddie had reluctantly decided that he did not possess Herculax's power, and he longed more eagerly than ever to see this god and perhaps learn the secret of his strange command.

But his father's words had given him an idea. He had to have the money, for he felt that, if he missed seeing Herculax, his life would ever afterwards have an awful empty feeling, like the day when he rose too late for breakfast and had to begin with dinner.

The idea had come to him in bed. He would earn the money. He had hardly been able to wait for the morning to come, and now it had come he was going to earn his ninepence. It would be easy. Herculax the mighty. He was going to see him. There was no man in the village of Barton so strong and wonderful.

The ground rose more steeply and was studded with thorn bushes that showed a covering of fresh green in emphatic contrast with the dark firs on the sky-line. He stood for a moment on the edge of the wood and looked back. Down in the valley was the village He could just see the edge of the square church tower behind the chestnuts and the lazy drift of smoke from the houses.

In the valley a mist lay which promised one of those blazing summer days that sometimes surprises the spring. The country smiled at the warm sky, and the rooks in the elms by the rectory made a great fuss as they inspected the damage done to their nests by the winter winds. But Freddie was scarcely conscious of it. Tomorrow the circus would have arrived, and Herculax would be ordering his animals about their den.

He was sure that if his father had been as magnificent as Herculax he would have given him ninepence. At that moment he could think of nothing more delightful than having a,man like Herculax for a father. The joy of the thought set his body wriggling and he could not keep still. He hurried into the wood.

As he went, young hazel boughs brushed at his hair and his feet made a hissing noise across the dead leaves that clustered in great drifts round the smooth trunks of the beeches. He left the path and climbed across the waste of rotting boughs and leaves. He did not stop for anything. He knew what he wanted and where to find it.

Through the dead leaves young spikes of garlic were pushing their way, and once a white spray of wayfaring tree in early bloom filled his nostrils with a sweet, sickening odour. On he moved, his feet crunching over the ground and his mind picturing Herculax cracking his whip and shouting at the crouching, snarling lions. He could see their tensed flanks and straining paws and the calm. unafraid look of Herculax poised like a god over them.

A jay discovered him and flew from tree to tree, cursing, and warning everything in the wood of his presence. Presently he came to a dip in the wood, a little dell sentinelled by dwarf may-bushes and thin ash poles that were just creaking bud. The floor of the dell was covered with a great pad of green and yellow primroses.

Freddie stopped. For a moment the glory and wonder of the flowers that were filling the air with their slight elusive scent drove Herculax from his mind. Then he was Freddie who wanted ninepence again. Here, in this dell, lay his ninepence; here, cradled in this mass of green and yellow freshness, was hidden the key which would bring him closer to Herculax, which would admit him into the circus tent to watch the springing lions, the snarling leopards, and the magnificent lion tamer.

Freddie set his basket down on the edge of the patch of flowers and began to pick. His hair fell into his eyes and his small hands were stained with the damp earth. When he judged that he had enough, he stopped, and sitting on the edge of the dell, drew from his pocket some. lengths of his father's raffia twine which he had taken from the tool-shed of the cottage.

With the twine he bound the primroses into generous bunches, twisting the raffia inexpertly round the downy stems, and apportioning to each bunch three broad leaves to protect the yellow blaze as he had seen the market women do. Within half an hour he had a dozen bunches lying in his basket.

He left the dell, climbed right through the wood, scrambled through the rough hedge at the top and then, after breasting the ridge, came down a narrow bridle path that served as the bed of a stream in winter to the main road. And it was here that be was going to earn his ninepence.

At a penny a bunch the primroses would bring him a shilling, which would give him threepence for sweets as well as the circus admission price. At a pinch he was prepared to forgo the sweets, but he did not anticipate that trade would be so bad. Surely, anyone from the City passing in a car would be glad to buy the flowers; they were so pretty.

He tidied the flowers from the shaking that they had received when he negotiated the hedge, and then he sat on the road fence and waited hopefully. For a long time nothing passed, but he did, not mind. It was a lovely day, summer-like, but full of spring clearness, and he was glad of the rest after his long climb and walk.

From where the road dipped out of sight over the hill brow there came the sound of a motor's engine. Freddie hopped from the fence excitedly. He was going to sell his flowers. He clutched the basket tightly to him and held up a bunch of primroses. The roar increased and suddenly a car shot over the rise and sped along the. rpad towards him. Freddie waved his flowers and shouted:

"Primroses!   Penny a bunch … Primroses!"

His last words were drowned in the noise of the car as it passed and disappeared He was disappointed. but his optimism buoyed him up. The driver was perhaps in a hurry to fetch a doctor or do something else, othenwise he must have stopped. Others would not be in so much haste, and he would have his ninepence and see

Herculax. The yellow flowers reminded him of the gold bangles on the lion-tamer's wrists, and, in the consequent reverie, Freddie let a car slip by without giving him time to flourish his flowers. He did not mind. There was plenty of time yet and the others would buy.

But the others did not buy.The day wore on and many cars passed along the road but none stopped. Either the occupants did not notice the tiny figure at the roadside or they did not want primroses. Time and again Freddie jumped from his fence and held aloft his flowers, but the only thing he received was a thin coating of dust from the whirring wheels. The day, fulfilling. the promise of the morning, grew hotter. The dust settled on his clothes, streaked his perspiring face with mild runnels of dirt and the primroses began to wilt and lose their freshness before the onslaught of sun and dust. And then, when his spirits were lowest, a car did stop. A thin-faced man, wearing spectacles, leaned out.

"Trade don't seem so good, sonny, does it?" he called. Freddie was too excited to reply immediately. Here was someone who wanted to buy. The vision of Herculax, which had been growing faint, developed a new life and colour.

"How much a bunch?" the man went on.

"Pen —" Freddie hesitated. He had intended to sell them at a penny, but he saw that he must alter his price if he wanted to earn ninepence. "Tuppence a bunch. mister."

The man smiled, took a bunch from him and handed him a threepenny-bit. "Keep the change." The car drove off.

Freddie was elated. He stared at the coin and then carefully tied it in the corner of his handkerchief. He was convinced now that he would soon have ninepence. But he did not soon have ninepence. Cars passed, petrol tankers, heavy lorries, little saloon cars, large expensive cars, and cyclists, but none of them stopped. Freddie grew dispirited. For the first time he felt the sting of the gorse scratches on his knees, and he wished that he had saved some of the bread and dripping his mother had given him for his lunch which he had eaten hours ago. The sun was overpoweringly hot and the road offered no shade.

His flowers grew limper and the fresh green of the leaves turned to a withered drabness, and his feet were uncomfortable where he had walked in the pools along the bridle path. His arm ached from holding up his flowers, and where he had once been

111

heartened by the thought of Herculax. he now found it harder to keep the lion-tamer in mind He tried to be brave, as brave as Herculax, but it was difficult People didn't want his primroses. It seemed unbelievable that, of all the people in cars who had passed, only one had wanted primroses. Didn't people know about primroses? At the end of the afternoon Freddie knew that he would never get his ninepence. He sat down on the road turf and bit his thumbnail to keep himself from letting his mouth quiver.

He had tried to earn the money. It seemed unfair that no one would help or understand. He wouldn't be able to see the mighty Herculax, no circus. He tried to recall those shiny, glossy biceps and muscles, that challenging look and the curling whip; but the memory now only hurt him. His nail left his mouth and his face puckered involuntarily.

"Hey, sonny! Stop snivelling and tell me where Barton is."

Freddie started. and looked up. A car had drawn silently alongside him, and a woman with a small, frowning face and cold eyes, was addressing him from the wheel. Her tone was far from cordial.

"I'm not snivelling." Freddie replied.

"Never mind about that! Is this the way to Barton?" snapped the woman.

"Barton's where I live"

"That's right — anything but what I want to know. I want to know if this is the way to Barton?"

"Down there."Freddie was too miserable to be annoyed at her asperity. He pointed down the road.

"Thank you." The woman turned and spoke sharply to a heavily-coated figure in the back of the car. "Give the brat something for telling us, though he's probably told us wrong."

A man moved forward from the back of the car and a coin was tossed towards Freddie. He scarcely saw the coin. He was staring at the man's face. Over a rigidly waxed moustache he met the eyes of Herculax. The whole world turned over and fell at Freddie's feet. The shilling lay in the dust unheeded. Herculax was before him, a living hero, a god who strode proudly among the animals. Nothing could equal this joy. Freddie stared until the car started with a jerk that sent Herculax back into his seat.

Herculax — if only he could grow up to be like him. Splendid, shining, unafraid, magnificent. Half dazed with the wonder of this visitation, Freddie bent for the shilling, and did not hear the woman snap to her companion as the car started:

"Now, perhaps we shall get somewhere. Why I married you I don't know! Herculax the Lion-Tamer! Huh! First you direct me wrongly, and then you waste our money by giving the lad a shilling. You're an idiot."

"Yes, my darling," came the subdued reply as Herculax settled back into the cushions.

A FRIEND OF THE FAMILY

Mellow, early September sunlight through the window; the aroma of eggs and bacon and freshly-ground coffee; in its little silver rack the toast, sliced to the right thickness, cut to the preferred shape and browned to just the right degree; the morning paper, folded, waiting to his hand on the table ...

Sir Hugh Dobson smiled. He had been away for three months. Now, on his first morning back home, everything was just as it had been, just as it should be. And also perhaps — the question brought a very slight, quizzical lift to the greying eyebrows over the faded blue eyes in his sun-tanned face — just as it always would be?

In ten years' time, when he would be sixty, would he be sitting here, enjoying the simple delights of a traditional breakfast and Mrs. Miller coming in and out, her movements regulated by some instinctive sense of timing and knowing when she was wanted?

Breakfast was a ceremony, life was a ritual, broken at times, but always there waiting to be resumed, nothing in fact ever really changing. Sir Hugh grinned again, but this time it was with a touch of cynicism. He shook the morning newspaper open and glanced at the front page headlines. Then he opened it to the Court page. For more years than he could remember he had always turned to the Court page.

His eyes ran over the page, surveying a domain in which he moved easily: names, honours and announcements, some passing without stir and many waking memories of a lifetime. An item caught his eye.

> ***Mr. G. A. Campbell and Miss D. M. Hapgood.***
> *The engagement is announced between George, youngest son of Mr. and Mrs. D. G. Campbell of Beath Lodge, Caithness, and Daphne, daughter of Mr. F. S. Hapgood of High Park, Oughton, Sussex and Mrs. Hapgood of Fir Bank, Toxton, Wilts.*

Well, well … so Daphne — his godchild — was, engaged. But who the devil was George Campbell? A Scot, clearly. Well, whoever he was, he would have to be right before Freddie Hapgood of High Park and the International Finance Trust gave him a warm welcome as a son-in-law.

Freddie had made his own millions and, in the process, had given Margaret at Fir Bank no option but to divorce him — which was exactly what he had wanted. Daphne was lovely and charming, but she was a chip off the old block. Very little of Margaret Hapgood there.

What kind of man was Daphne going to settle for? By God, he would have to be right. Daphne was all woman, but she was never going to be anyone's doormat, like her mother.

Sir Hugh sat back and thought about Margaret. For a while his memories and the steady nostalgia of his own love for her made him neglect his breakfast. A sudden, impish sense of humour lit his distinguished face as he acknowledged to himself that there wasn't another woman in the world who could make him let his eggs go cold. He must tell Margaret that sometime. It was the kind of observation she delighted in … this weekend, maybe, while he was down.

Sir Hugh spent a busy morning at the Treasury, shaped and put in order his reports on his last trip abroad. At lunchtime he went round to his club in St. James's Street and, as he knew he would, found Freddie Hapgood sitting in the Long Bar.

Freddie was a dark-haired cumbersome man, his whole appearance a manifestation of clumsy, thrusting power. Their friendship was based less on liking than mutual respect, and there had never been anything but frankness between them.

Sir Hugh sat down with him and the club servant brought him his usual drink.

Freddie said: "Good trip?"

Sir Hugh grinned. "You wouldn't think so — wasting the public's money on incompetent, underdeveloped countries."

"Damn right. You Whitehall people are all the same. Hear about Daphne?"

"Yes. Who's this George Campbell?"

Freddie stirred, shaking his big shoulders. "Who is he? I'll tell you — damn all! He's a would-be Napoleon in windbreaker and faded denims."

Sir Hugh chuckled. "Sounds like a past description of you, Freddie."

"Exactly." For a moment Freddie smiled and there was a sudden boyishness that was disarming. "That's why I don't like him. The world hasn't got room for the two of us in one family."

"Father-in-law afraid of a takeover?"

"Father-in-law isn't afraid of anyone, as you know. I'm thinking of Daphne — she may have a tiger by the tail."

"Just like Margaret had with you?"

"Yes. And damn your frankness."

"Beath Lodge, Caithness — what's that? Some crumbling old castle with twenty thousand acres of useless moorland, lochs and mountains?"

Freddie snorted "Beath Lodge is two down and three up, outside loo and well-water. George, Campbell's father, is a gamekeeper and, I'll give him this, he doesn't mind a damn who knows it." He rose. "Got a lunch date. You're Daphne's godfather — can't think why I asked you — but have a chat with her. Talk her out of this. She's no tiger tamer."

Sir Hugh was far from agreeing with him. There were more ways of taming men and tigers than by using brute force. One thing Daphne had which her father would never possess was an understanding of people's weaknesses, knowing they often covered the foundations of real strength.

Before going in to lunch, Sir Hugh called Daphne at her Chelsea boutique and asked her down to the country for the weekend.

Late on Friday afternoon, Sir Hugh went down to Hampshire. Mrs. Miller had gone down in the morning to open up the house. It was a small Georgian house on the banks of the River Test and had been in Sir Hugh's family for over a hundred years. Most of his boyhood had been spent there.

Shortly after he had arrived Sir Hugh did what he always did if the season was right. He took his fly rod and walked down to the river. Swallows were hawking low over the water and under a willow on the far bank a trout was rising to a hatch of flies.

116

Sir, Hugh knew the trout — a cock fish called Hannibal which he had been trying to catch for three years. Purely as a formal greeting to an old enemy, Sir Hugh made half-a-dozen casts to Hannibal who ignored his offering while gulping away at a natural fly. Sir Hugh moved on to easier prey and returned to the house with a couple of trout for the next day's breakfast. He fixed himself a drink and went through the mail which had accumulated. Only one letter really interested him. It was from Margaret Hapgood, who lived about forty miles away. It read:

Dear Hughie,
    Dinner, Monday the seventh, usual time. Missed your help on the WI stall summer fete. We took £150, a record, and Brown's boy broke his leg on the toboggan slide. D's getting engaged. I like him, but query, query and will discuss.

Love, M.

Sir Hugh smiled. She wrote as she talked. Staccato, bird-like. A warm, friendly woman with a life full of lame dogs and stiles. He had loved her before Freddie had married her and loved her still, wanting no other woman.

Every seventh of September, since the divorce, they had dined together and over his port he had always asked her to marry him and had always been refused. Forty-three ... Good God, she was still a young woman by today's reckoning, and she looked like one. She took as good care of herself as she did of the people who came to her for help. Brown's boy, he grinned, would have a ward bed littered with her books.

He met Daphne at the station the next morning and brought her back to the house. They sat on the terrace in the sunshine and had pre-lunch drinks. Daphne was twenty-four, blonde like her mother, and with the same oval face, almost Scandinavian good looks. A thoroughbred. Always had been difficult to school, but with an innate sense of self-discipline.

Sitting with her feet stretched out on another chair, Daphne raised her glass to him. "Well ... what does godfather have to say? I know the meaning of those three rather attractive wrinkles between your eyes."

"Congratulations, of course. And, thank God, someone else is going to take you off my hands. I hope you will be very happy."

"Oh, I shall — but I'll have to work at it. Just like the boutique. With George, it's not enough to fall in love. That's just the dream to build on."

"Tell me about George."

"Oh, I forgot to say. He's driving me back to town. I said you'd give him lunch if he could make it."

"Naturally. Now tell me about him."

"A rough sketch. He loves talking about himself so I won't cramp his style. Let's see — he's medium height, solid. Nice brown eyes that can go mad if you cross him. Very strong, wilful, ambitious — but then again, when you least expect it, he's surprisingly gentle and understanding. Poor boy, father a gamekeeper, and then all the usual — scholarships, university, ambition and, thank God, a sense of humour.

"It's purely a question of timing whether he finishes up a millionaire or doing a ten-year stretch in prison. And, of course, I love him. Freddie is baffled by him, and Mother thinks he doesn't look after himself ..."

"And what does this protean young man do?"

Daphne finished her drink and held out her glass to be refilled. "He moves earth."

"He what?"

"Moves earth. Or his men do. Billions of tons of it. All those piles you see when they make new roads and clear building sites."

"And he makes money?"

"Not enough. But he will. Capital is his big problem."

Sir Hugh eyed her quizzically. She was a wealthy girl in her own right from a substantial legacy left by her grandmother.

Daphne read his thoughts, "The answer," she said, "is — no. He won't take a penny from me. He says that's one obligation no man must be under to his wife." She sipped her drink and then said slowly and seriously: "You'll like him, but I should warn you ... he'll try and shock you some way or another. It's a thing he's got — well, I suppose, to emphasise that he's moving under his own steam. Sir Hugh Dobson is a natural target. Just for the hell of it he'll want to knock you off balance."

Sir Hugh laughed. "Fascinating. I can't wait."

118

George Campbell arrived the next day at mid-morning. He drove an old and very dirty family saloon and wore a shapeless suede jacket and blue denims. His Scottish accent was muted and the wry, pugnacious set of his features was contradicted by the warmth and humour of his eyes — which missed nothing.

While they were having drinks before lunch, Daphne left them to go and help Mrs. Miller. George nodded after her and said, "Tactful lass, Sir Hugh. Left us alone for catechism time — so fire away."

Sir Hugh said blandly: "I wasn't thinking of asking any questions."

"But I'd like you to. You're the great Sir Hugh, right-hand man of the P.M. Confidential government emissary. And Daphne thinks the world of you."

Sir Hugh said: "Do you love her?"

"Yes, I do."

Sir Hugh said bluntly: "How do you know?"

A look of surprise moved in George's eyes and then he grinned. "Good question. I love her because from the first moment I saw her I knew that everything I did from that moment included her as vitally as every breathing second of my life must include air. But," and the brown eyes flickered humorously, "I'd like that kept confidentially between us. If she knew she'd make capital from it and get out of hand. Next?"

Sir Hugh shook his head. "No more. Did you know that you were paraphrasing Elizabeth Barrett Browning? *What I do and what I dream include thee, as the wine must taste of its own grapes?*"

"Aye, I did. *If thou must love me, let it be for naught — except for love's sake only.* And now, since you are clearly a man of substance, Sir Hugh, would you be interested in investing a few thousands in a young and growing business with unlimited opportunities?"

"Yours, of course?"

"Naturally."

Sir Hugh laughed. "Oh dear, I can see why Freddie doesn't want you in the family. You know, of course, that I'm a Treasury man? I don't fool around with money, particularly my own. Send me a detailed analysis of your last year's business and a projection —

119

with sound reasons — of your estimate of development over the next three. I'll consider it."

"My God — that's the way I like to hear a man talk business. Aye, and my name's not George Campbell if you don't approve. Do I strike you as brash, arrogant?"

"I gather that's what you intend. Come, I'll show you another of your kind ... named after a conqueror who didn't know the meaning of No."

He took George down to the river where Hannibal was rising leisurely now and then to feed.

George watched the trout and said: "Yon's a bonnie fish. But there's no kingdom ever yet secure against some attack or other. Let him make one slip and there's always another trout to take his place in the scheme of things."

During a lull in lunch, Daphne looked across at Sir Hugh and said: "Has George tried to borrow any money from you yet, Hughie?"

As George smiled, Sir Hugh said easily: "No — but he has pointed out a possible investment opening for me."

Daphne turned to George. "George, you promised!"

"Aye, I did — and I kept it. Not borrowing but investing — two different things. When you lay down a condition, my darling, you should pick your words with care or the contract is meaningless. Right, Sir Hugh?"

"Absolutely," Hugh chuckled.

Daphne said to George: "I'll speak to you in the car."

George nodded. "Why not? That routine is a part of all true marriages." Then: "Tell me, sir, what is your honest opinion of Masterson?"

For a fraction of a second Sir Hugh felt himself off balance. To make a frank reply about a Government Minister like Masterson was completely alien to his nature. But seeing George's eyes on him, knowing there was a uniqueness in thus young man that he was still fighting to control and use for his own good, he said bluntly for him: "He's a man of an ambivalent nature."

George laughed. "Aye, well put and what I expected. But I prefer the common touch. The man's an incompetent fathead and a dishonest one." He reached over and held Daphne's hand gently and went on: "Your father doesn't like me — and I can't say I blame him. Your mother's a honey and puts on rose-coloured spectacles when she sees me.

"But your godfather now ... he's everything I would like to become and know I never shall — a man of grace and subtlety. Me, I'm strictly a reality man. Pounds, shillings and pence and a warm bed with the woman you love in it."

Daphne turned to Sir Hugh and raised her eyebrows questioningly. "Do you think I should call the whole thing off?"

Sir Hugh rose. "No. Let him run. Life will smooth the rough edges in time."

He left them with their coffee alone on the terrace and went up to his room to glance through the Sunday papers. After a while he dozed off in his armchair. He awoke an hour later and went to the window.

Across the lawns by the river he could see George fly-fishing. He used a fly rod as though he had had one in his hands since the time he could walk.

A strange young man, George. Self-made and still ambitiously self-making and he had little time to spare for making people like him. No airs, no graces, no diplomacy — but the time for that would come later. That's where Daphne would come into her own.

Half an hour later as Sir Hugh and Daphne sat having tea on the terrace, George came up from the river, fly rod in one hand and a fish in the other.

"Look at this, Sir Hugh. Your friend Hannibal. Five pounds if he's an ounce — and he fought like a tiger." He laid the fish on the glass-topped terrace table.

Sir Hugh looked down at the fish. The sunlight gilded the firm flanks like old gold and the scarlet and brown spots stood out boldly. For a moment there was a sense of loss. For years he had known Hannibal.

Quietly he said: "Well done, George. What fly did you use?"

George shook his head. "No fly, Sir Hugh. He'd look at none. So — like any gamekeeper's boy — I found a worm and flicked it to him. He took it first go and —"

"George!" Daphne broke in angrily: "How could you? For God's sake, this is the Test, the finest trout stream in the country — and you know damn well it's fly only! And you know even more damn well that Sir Hugh will never forgive you for using a worm!" She turned away, her eyes blazing.

George looked at Sir Hugh and said quietly: "Fly only. Aye, I know that. It's the ritual. But the reality is there, a bonnie fish ready for the pot. Am I to be forgiven, Sir Hugh?"

For a moment Sir Hugh said nothing. For all his liking of this young man, there was an anguish in him, a deep concern, not only for George, but for Daphne and George together. He wondered if Daphne would ever work out why George went out of his way to create new obstacles for himself.

He said stiffly: "When you send me that analysis you've promised I shall expect also a letter of apology for this. I promise to give you a prompt answer to both communications."

He turned from George, put his hand on Daphne's shoulder and said to her: "I've got some work I must do. Come and say goodbye to me in the study before you go."

He walked away.

Hardly a word passed between them on the drive back to London. When George pulled up outside Daphne's flat, he turned to her and said, smiling: "Nice to drive in silence sometimes. Gives a man time to think. I liked Sir Hugh."

"You don't mean you like him — you mean you're happy about him because you think he'll come across with some cash. Just at the moment, I hate your guts, George Campbell."

"It'll pass, darling. And I mean I like him."

"Then why that stupid worm business?"

"The object was to make him remember me, and understand me. Liking comes after that. He knows that I get what I want, even if I have to be unorthodox about it. For God's sake — if you're going to put money in a man's business that's something you've got to know."

He leaned over and kissed her on the cheek. "Love's one thing, liking's another — but business is business, and success is the thing that pays the bills, buys the dresses, the smart cars and lets people sleep warm at night without too many cares."

Daphne said quietly: "I ought to get out of this car and walk right out of your life. At one moment today I thought I would."

"Then why didn't you?"

"For two reasons. The first you know."

"And the second?"

"Because of something Hughie said to me before we left."

"And what was that?"

"Oh, no — I'm not going to make it easy for you." She leaned forward and kissed him gently on the lips. "One day I'll tell you — but you've got a lot of growing up to do first. Don't be too long about it, Georgie boy."

It was a calm, warm evening and through the, open windows the evening air made the flames of the candles waver gently and throw liquid reflections across the polished tables and the dinner silver.

It was the seventh of September, and as Sir Hugh fingered the stem of his port glass, he had a feeling that this year things would be different ... Daphne was as good as off Margaret's hands now.

Margaret said: "I'm glad you've met George at last. You know how much I depend on you, Hughie. Weak me." She smiled. "Until I have your verdict I've got none of my own."

"I wonder ..." He sipped his port and went on, "Anyway — I like him. He's got character and good qualities. But at the moment he's all at sea.

"His problem is the same as any new boy going to school for the first time. You either stay quietly in the background until you become accepted as part of the system — or you decide on being an exhibitionist, and take a chance on whether you are finally accepted or ignored.

"George is the exhibitionist, but of a rare kind. He only pretends to break the rules." He chuckled. "Oh, yes, he's clever. He always leaves himself a way out if things should go wrong. I told you about his taking Hannibal with a worm, didn't I?"

"Yes. Unforgivable."

"Of course. But he lied about it. I was watching him through glasses from my room. He took Hannibal on a fly — completely orthodox and most beautifully and skilfully done."

"Then why did he tell you —?"

"That's what Daphne wanted to know. The answer's simple. George is ambitious, clever — and uncertain. With success, and with Daphne's help, he'll grow out of it. Oh, there'll be twice-monthly fireworks for a while between them, but in the end I see no reason why they shouldn't end up with a relationship that a lot of marriages never achieve."

"You make him sound like another Freddie."

"Oh no. Freddie would have used a worm and sworn that he used a fly." Sir Hugh paused, then he stretched out his hand and rested it on hers. "But I don't want to talk about George or Freddie. Freddie's gone, and Daphne is off your hands. Now there's just you and me —"

"And always the same question between us?"

"Yes, my dear. Always."

She said quietly: "Hughie, I'm going to be frank with you. And don't get cross with me. If you really loved me I know I would have fallen in love with you."

"Margaret, how can you —"

"No, listen. You were sorry for me when the Freddie thing happened. You were wonderful to me. And you took Daphne under your wing. And once a year, we've sat here, going through our little ritual. But, Hughie, darling, that's all it is."

"Nonsense. I love you."

"No you don't. You love the idea of loving me. You're the perfect courtier. You give the lady what you think she wants. But there's nothing the lady can give you, Hughie. I want a love that comes from needing and necessity on both sides, from my own and someone else's weakness. The thing in fact that you say George and Daphne have."

She drew her hand from his and stood up. "The ritual is over, Hughie. This is the last time. Please don't miss it too much. You see — I'm going to be married to a man of half your character who loves and needs me."

From a numbness of spirit Sir Hugh heard himself say: "Who?"

"Brigadier Gerson. Retired. You know him?"

"Vaguely. Good chap. Never did much, though."

Margaret laughed. "Oh, Hughie — how like you."

She came round the table, leaned over him and kissed him on the temple.

"You really mean this, Margaret? That all these years you think I've played the part I felt was demanded of me?"

"Yes, I do, my dear. And beautifully." She smiled down at him. "I don't think you knew you were doing it. And don't look so cast down, Hughie. Let me tell you something — in a little while you're going to be feeling relieved. You're free. Now ..." she moved away from him, "you finish your port. You can join me for coffee."

Sir Hugh stood and watched her leave the room. Through the open casement came the call of an evening blackbird and an early bat zigzagged across the lawns. He crossed the room and looked out into the darkening garden.

For a moment he felt that he could be angry, felt sorry for himself, and then slowly the impulse faded. He breathed the cool night air and suddenly a rare feeling of relief swept over him and slowly he began to chuckle to himself. The freedom he had not known he wanted lay wide before him.

THE DAFFODIL DAY

Sam Hearn sat on the long bench which ran the length of the trestle table set up in the garden of the country café. His little club coach party of 'Oldies' — Senior Citizens' Circle officially — had taken their tea in the bright April sunshine and had now wandered off into the nearby wood to admire the great stretches of wild daffodils that coated the ground under the trees like a golden carpet. They were a nice bunch and he liked them all, and every year, on the day before Good Friday, they came over for what was known as 'Daffodil Day.' Normally he would have gone into the wood with them, but today his spirits were low and his thoughts none too happy.

All the way over from Warkham his right shoulder had been troubling him, giving him more pain then he had known before. If it got worse he knew that he would have to think about giving up coach driving. And once he did that … what on earth would he do about a job? He didn't know. There was a tight little knot of apprehension in him which could not be ignored. At fifty-eight he'd be on the scrap heap. Jobs — particularly for a man with a gammy shoulder — didn't come two-a-penny these days. Thank God, anyway, he had only himself to look after … though that was poor comfort.

A shadow fell across him and he looked up to see a young man standing before him. He had a pleasant face, rather longish hair, wore a pale brown sort of kaftan affair and open-work sandals on his feet. Hippy-type, thought Sam, no care in the world, just drifting and living day by day as it came, and always on the watch for a hand-out.

The young man said, "I see from the sign on your coach that you're from Warkham."

"That's right." There was little grace in Sam's tones.

"I was wondering if you would be kind enough to give me a lift there?"

"You're not backward in coming forward, are you?"

"I suppose not. Would you mind?"

It was on the tip of Sam's tongue to say No when to his surprise he heard himself say, "Well, I suppose so. We're far from full up today."

"That's kind of you. Is your shoulder hurting you very much?"

"How do you know about that?"

The young man laughed. "I've been watching you — plucking up courage to ask for a lift. Do you mind, perhaps I can help?" Without waiting for a reply the young man put his hands on Sam's shoulder and began to massage and manipulate it. For a moment Sam would have pulled away, but then he relaxed and let the young man have his way — and, in a little while, he realised that it was a good way. He felt the stiffness ease from him and the nagging pain slowly depart.

Sam said gratefully, "My goodness — you've really got something, haven't you?"

"It's just a knack. But it'll come back, you know … though not for quite a while."

"That's what worries me. What will I do then? No driving. On the scrap heap. However, luckily, there's only me. My wife's dead and my only son is well set-up in Australia … married, a family. Anyway, why am I telling you all this?"

"Because troubles shrink when they're shared?"

"Maybe. Anyway — thank you very much. And now, here comes my party. I'll tell them you're joining us. They won't mind. They're a nice lot."

Looking at the little party coming out of the mood the young man said, "None of them have picked any daffodils."

Sam smiled. "No, they never do. It's enough for them just to come and enjoy them where God put them. I should warn you that we always have a bit of a sing-song on the way back. Mr. Alsop plays his mouth-organ for it. He was a Sergeant-Major in the Infantry during the war. A real fire-eater."

It was a jolly returning party, Sam Hearn drove without any pain from his shoulder, and late Sergeant-Major Alsop played his mouth-organ to accompany the singing. Sam had introduced the young man to them and they all gave him a friendly welcome. When it was over Mr. Alsop came and sat by the young man and said, "Did you enjoy that, lad?"

"Very much."

"Aye, nothing like a good tune to put heart and spirit into the troops. Many a time before going into the thick of it I've pulled out the old mouth-organ and given the lads a rouser. Into battle with a song in your hearts — that's the way. Put your faith in God all right — but there's nothing like a bit of music to keep the spirits up. Ah, yes — I remember just before an attack at Cassino, Italy that was, long before your time ..." He broke off and looked hard at the young man and then, in a mild voice, said, "Now, isn't that strange — I was going to spin you a good old fairy tale of a yarn."

The young man smiled. "I know you were. And I'm sorry to have missed it. The gift of story-telling is a great one, and I'm sure you have it. You wanted to be a hero, didn't you? And given the chance you would have been. There's nothing wrong with dreams so long as in the telling of them we don't convert them into facts. What were you?"

Hardly able to believe that it was his own voice, Mr. Alsop said, "Royal Army Service Corps. Never heard a shot fired in anger the whole war. Stomach ulcers."

"Well, fighting men have to eat. All men serve, one way or another. Not that I approve of war."

"Who does in his heart?"

When Mr. Alsop went back to sit with his wife she said, with a small smile, "I suppose you've been telling him all your war adventures?"

"As a matter of fact, no,"

"Are you feeling well?"

"Of course I am ..." He paused, and then went on almost to himself, "You know, there's something funny about him. I was going to spin him a pack of lies — and then suddenly I couldn't,"

"Well, that's a change."

Almost to himself Mr. Alsop said, "Yes ... I think it is. Odd, very odd."

Other people on that trip back to Warkham found the young man talking to them either as he sat by them or stood swaying gently in the seat aisle. He seemed to come and go with a naturalness that none of them questioned as odd.

Miss Dora Ashwell, a long retired musical comedy actress, comfortably off — for all her life she had been careful with her money — found him standing in the aisle alongside her and, being a

128

forthright character, said, "I can't think why you young men these days have to wear such weird clothes. You look as though you're half-dressed for a part in *The Desert Song* or an Aladdin panto." And then, giving him a warm smile, she said, "Don't mind me. I always speak first and think afterwards."

He smiled. "I think more people should do that. The truth comes easier that way. Do you miss the bright lights and the stage?"

"Oh, I see Soldier Boy Alsop has been giving you the gossip on us all. And the answer is — no I don't. Not like my sister in London — we had a sister act you know. She's always pining for the past — but never had the sense to save for her old age. She's not well off and I've often thought of asking her to live with me, but I just couldn't stand it. It would be Do-you-remember-such-and-such? And, I'll never-forget-that-night-we-all-sent-out-to-dinner-after-the-opening-at-Blackpool. On and on — while the potatoes are boiling over or the roast is burning."

"Perhaps it's because she's got so little in the present that she clings to the past. While you've got your little house and garden and are perfectly happy?"

"How could you know that?"

He laughed and smiled and she thought that the look on his face was at once merry and wise. He said, "I didn't. I just guessed. You know some people know how to look after themselves — and others need looking after. Put the two together and sometimes the result can be very rewarding."

"Not with my sister, my dear boy."

As he moved on from Miss Dora Ashwall a man reached out from a seat and plucked at his sleeve.

"Come and sit downs feller-me-lad. Seeing you swaying about like that makes me giddy." As the young man sat down, he went on, "Gould's the name. Ginger Gould they called me when these —" he touched his grey-white hair, "— were copper coloured instead of off-white and far fewer of 'em. I been watching you. You a reporter or something, going round chatting people up? Easter Outing. Nice little piece for the local paper or something? Well, you'll get nothing from me that'll make the headlines." He laughed brightly. "My life wouldn't make news. Nearer eighty than seventy now. Into service when I was thirteen. Boot boy. Then pantry boy. Fetching coals, lighting fires. Winter mornings a sight more biting than they ever are

129

these days. Bright I was though, and ambitious. Give me anything mechanical from a sewing machine to a musical box and I could make it work. And motors …! Oh, I tell you, young man, I fell in love with them. Chauffeur-gardener in the end. Guess for how many years?"

"Right up to the day you retired?"

"Dead right. And the same family all through! Knew His Lordship as a boy. Same age as me. Into mischief together. But no over-stepping the line. Drove him, I did, when he came into the title. And drove him, I did, when he was put away seven years ago. Had it in his will, he did. That I was to drive the hearse. And drive it I did. Service. That's a dirty word these days. They have to sneer when they say it. But I say service is the true destiny of a man … in high or low degree, whichever God has called him to. Talk a lot, don't I? But I don't mind. All this lot know me and they just tell me to shut up or go and sit somewhere else. All nice people. In fact, most people is nice if you get the right spot to view 'em from. What do you do for a living?"

"Well … I'm sort of between situations at the moment. I expect the family left you well provided for — being such an old retainer?"

"They were fair, and I saved. Wife's gone now and the children all away and settled."

"So you want for nothing?"

Ginger Gould laughed. "Don't you believe it. Man always wants for something here below. I want to grow better onions then the chap next door — though I don't think I ever will. I want to win the pools. No luck so far. I went the council to come and fix my roof that leaks — been waiting four months, I have. But most of all I want my cat back."

"Tell me about the cat."

"There's nowt to tell. Had her four years and she's just walked out on me. Week ago. Miss her I do. But I'm sensible about it. Cats come and go. Lots of things can happen to 'em. So it can to humans. Here today, gone tomorrow. But that's the way. All you can do is live straight, keep yourself tidy, be civil to your neighbours, say your prayers and don't keep late hours. And like His Lordship used to say — when you get up in the morning praise God for a new day, and when you go to bed at night give Him thanks for its safe passing. And now, if you really want to do someone a favour and got

130

something for your newspaper piece, go and talk to Miss Elliston up the back there. She'd love to be in a newspaper piece. She loves famous people. Keeps a cutting book about 'em. She almost saw the Queen once. She came to open a new hospital near Warkham. But just as the royal car began to come up the drive she fainted with excitement. They lifted her out over everyone's heads."

The young man laughed and then leaving Mr. Gould drifted to the back of the coach where he was greeted with a bright, friendly smile from Miss Elliston, a neat little women in a grey costume and wearing a saucy little straw hat with a blue ribbon around it which matched her bright, friendly eyes. As he sat down by her she said, "I know that Ginger Gould sent you up here. I saw him nod towards me. He's a great tease, you know. Are you from a paper, doing a piece perhaps for Easter? That's what we all think."

"Well, no — not anything like that. I just wanted a lift to Warkham and ... well, I like talking to people." He smiled. "He said you almost saw the Queen once."

"Oh, dear. Don't talk about it. The shame. And being lifted over the heads of the crowd. Thank goodness I don't remember anything about it."

"It must have been very disappointing for you. Why do you like famous people?"

"Well ... it's natural, isn't it? If you're nothing yourself it's exciting to see in the flesh someone who is. Do you think there's anything wrong with that?"

"No, I don't." He laughed. "But it's a good idea not to faint when the moment comes."

Miss Elliston was silent for a moment or two and then said, "I hope you won't mind me saying this, but I don't normally like the young people of today who dress ... well, the way you do. But on you it seems absolutely right."

"Thank you." He was silent for a moment and then said, "Tell me — why do you really want to meet someone famous?"

She was thoughtful for a while and then rather hesitantly said, "Well ... I suppose because of my diary. I've always kept one since a girl, but I never seem to have anything really interesting to put in it. I've lived a sheltered, quiet life. Father left me enough money for comfort. My diary is like my life, really. Just straightforward and ordinary. Oh ... I'd like just one really exciting thing to happen —

like the Queen, or anybody else famous just saying a word to me. And then — that would really be a red-letter day. And I'd enter it up in my diary in red ink instead of blue." She laughed, a little embarrassed. "Aren't I stupid?"

"No. I don't think so. And you never know … each morning that the sun comes up begins a red-letter day for someone. That is if they have the right kind of eyes to recognise it."

"Oh, I'll recognise it when it comes. I'll turn a corner one day and — bump — I'll walk right into someone famous and then —" she laughed, "— I'll find I've left my autograph book at home!"

When they reached Warkham they all said their goodbyes and separated to their homes. The evening was drawing in and the setting sun was reddening the western sky.

In his little house Ginger Gould lit his fire and began to prepare his supper, humming gently to himself. When it was done he sat down and opened his evening bottle of beer. As he took his first sip there was a scratching and bumping at the cat flap of the garden door and then into the room came his straying cat. She walked across to him, dropped a little bundle at his feet, and then went out again. The operation was repeated three times, and each time a kitten was brought to him. Mr. Gould watched in wonder and joy, and gave three or four deep, unmanly sniffs to keep the tears from his eyes.

At that moment, too, unusual things were happening around Warkham. Mr. Alsop, watching his wife as she reached for her apron to begin cooking their super, said — without knowing he was going to — "You needn't bother with that, me dear. You need a break from feeding the troops. I thought we'd walk across to the Golden Keys and have dinner there. Finish off the day proper. After all, I may not be able to cook a meal for the best little women in the world, but I can darned well buy her one now and again. And no argument — that's an order from a superior officer."

And Miss Dora Ashwell, in her comfortable, but over large for her alone, house, poured herself a second glass of sherry and suddenly found the prospect of the long evening alone an unpleasant one. Telly was company, but not human company. She found herself on her feet and going to the telephone, saying to herself, 'All right, we'll quarrel — but we always did. But she'll go to pot unless I look after her. And, maybe, I'll go to pot, too. Two's company — and we'll have rows. But what's wrong with a good row? Bucks you

132

both up.' She reached for the telephone and began to dial her sister's London number. As she did so she said aloud, grinning, "The Ashwell Sisters, together again in their astounding dance and song ensemble ..." Then, with a faint groan, she added, "Oh, Gawd, I hope I'm doing the right thing ..."

And at this moment Sam Hearn's landlady called up to him that he was wanted on the telephone. He went down and on the far end of the line, distorted a little with crackle but recognisable, came the voice of his son in Australia, saying, "Now Dad, I'm coming straight to the point and I don't want any argy-bargy about this. I'm doing well out here and Nell and me have talked it over. Wouldn't raise your hopes before, but now I can. You're coming out here for good — I'll fix it all ..." Oddly, as the talk went on, and through the surge of emotion in him, Mr. Hearn found himself thinking that his son's acquired Australian accent was even more pronounced than it had been when he had telephoned at Christmas.

As Sam Hearn talked to his son, Miss Elliston sat at the partly open window of her bed-sitting room overlooking the Warkham Churchyard with its row of ancient yews, hearing faintly the sound of the choir practising their Easter hymns coming through the calm evening air. Her diary lay open before her, waiting to be filled with her day's entry, and at its side lay a well used copy of the Bible. She always liked to read a little in it before she began to write, opening the Bible at random. She did so now and it came open at a well-known illustration of Christ and His disciples standing beside the Sea of Galilee. She looked at it and a queer feeling suddenly trickled slowly the length of her spine. Then she pulled herself together and scolded herself for her fancifulness. But, her eyes going to the churchyard at this moment, she saw clear in the dying light of the day the young man of the coach walking through the churchyard, his back to her, but the lights from the church windows picking him out clearly. Then he was gone, disappearing behind the line of the pathway yews.

She sat for a long while, unmoving. Then she opened her diary to begin to write up the day's event, choosing from her little set of coloured biros, not the blue one she always used, but a red one.

THROUGH THE EYES OF LOVE

Mr. James Jago came out of his hotel and walked, relishing the balm and brightness of an early spring morning, up the short pathway to the broad esplanade of Plymouth Hoe. Jimmy, he told himself, it's a great morning, the kind of morning when, if a man has but eyes to see them, the bright blossoms of happiness flourish on every tree and bush and the golden flash of unexpected opportunities show around every corner; a great morning, my boy, to be back in your old home town for the first time since you left it at the age of seventeen. Welcome back, Jimmy, welcome back. Not, of course, mind you, old boy, that we intend to stay long ... just long enough for the tears of sentiment to run dry and shaky finances restored, then on again with restless feet and a blithe heart. Though, the good Lord knows, old boy, at sixty perhaps it's time to begin thinking of settling down somewhere.

With a shrug of his shoulders he pushed this last thought from him. James Jago was adept at dismissing unpleasant thoughts. He walked slowly down the length of the Hoe, the sun gilding the waters of the Sound, the flash of gulls' wings cutting arabesques against the cliffs and green headlands of the wide curving bay and the air sharp with the salt of the sea. He was a tall, well-built man, his hat set at a modest angle of jauntiness, the light dove-grey coat with its dark velvet collar an impeccable fit and scrupulously brushed, and his shoes shining like ebony. He had a pleasant, square face, tanned by the suns of many countries, brown, merry eyes like polished filberts, and strong white teeth which were still all his own. Look good, look prosperous and the whole world is your oyster was Jimmy's motto.

When he came to Drake's statue half-way down the esplanade he stopped, lit a cheroot, and then gave a nod to the old sea-captain. Just so had the boy Jimmy all those years ago stood and given the bluff old pirate and adventurer a nod on the day he had left, his birth town, thinking then as the man thought now, stay at home and moss grows under your feet ... spread your sails, take wing and the world is there for plundering. Well, here he was back, and there was the old admiral, stout, sturdy, the weathered bronze face staring still seaward. Any regrets, Jimmy, he asked himself? Not a one … well, maybe a few, but none of any great account. West countrymen, the ones with fire in their bellies, had always been pirates, captains and adventurers.

He moved on to the end of the Hoe and came down on to the coast road by the towering citadel, the camellias in bloom still around its great gate. Below the road — a different place now — was the old bathing place at Tinside where his father used to drag him on spring and summer mornings to swim, a scrawny boy who hated getting up early and hated more the chill sea water. Health fad was dad, a daily dip in the briny would add years to your life. Not his, though. A German bomb had blasted poor old dad to paradise on the same night as the pier had been destroyed, and Mum, rest her soul, had followed soon after. School holiday mornings he had been dragged up here, and what had be got for it? Just a strong dislike of sea bathing … well, perhaps not just that. There had been Kathy.

As he strolled down the hill past the citadel, he mused, face it old man it's not sentiment for the old place that has brought you back. It's Kathy … and the unfading memory of first love, of a blue-eyed, fair-haired girl. And face it, old man, since the only person you're ever honest with is yourself, it's not just the memory of first love, the nostalgia for the young, gawky days of youth alone — it's really the driving of that old devil necessity. Kathy now was a widow and wealthy … a gold mine somehow be exploited. No need for decisions yet. He would know which road to travel after he had had lunch with her today. Just for the moment he was once more the young boy, his father gone straight off to work after bathing, walking back home, dark hair still sea damp, rolled towel and bathing dress under his arm.

Cheroot smoke shredding in the wind behind him, he walked down the slope of Madeira Road and on to the Barbican, but he walked not as a man of sixty, but as a boy of fourteen on the early summer morning when he had first seen Katherine Trent. That morning now was as fresh in his mind as though it had only happened yesterday. Carts, vans, and handbarrows lined up outside the fish quay where the gulls wheeled and called above the boats being unloaded; the old houses and inns fronting the oily, refuse-littered waters of Cattewater basin, many of them older by far than the famous steps where the Pilgrims embarked on the Mayflower; catches from the fishing boats spread across the slabs of the quayside ... mackerel, herring, flounder, dab, skate, ray, gurnard ... the morning full of bustle, shouting, carts rattling and he, Jimmy, dreaming along caught in his own private spell of voyaging and adventuring in far off lands. As he had wandered along watching the fish boxes being hauled ashore from the boats' holds, he had bumped into Katherine Trent and knocked the basket of fish she was carrying out of her hand.

He chuckled to himself now at the memory of a tall girl of his own age, wearing a blue-and-white striped straw hat, wide brimmed, and with a ribbon round it as blue as her eyes and the first words he ever had from her still able to make music in his memory.

"Whyn't you look where you're going, you clumsy dafty?"

Blushing and confused, he bent to rescue the spilled whiting which lay in the dust, wiping them with his bathing towel while she stood above him, unmoving, holding the basket like a queen while he filled it with his tribute.

So it had begun with no word from him except a mumbled 'Sorry' and then each morning after came the agony of looking for her only to get a cold stare for his faint nod until the day came when, with a smile she spoke to him again, coming up behind him with a heavy basket of live lobsters and saying 'Since you're going my way I don't mind you help me with these.'

And so, heart thumping, he did, a half an hour out of his way, the basket swinging between them into the town to the small restaurant her father ran and not a thought in his head that he would be late for school and caned.

Aye, Jimmy, he told himself as he strolled the length of the Barbican and the Parade to the Customs House and back, those were the days, the days of young love, the days that stretched to three years and made his dreams of travel and adventure fade, days when he saw everything through the eyes of love. Who would believe it? He'd worked nights in the restaurant while school lasted and then full time when he had left school. And all for the sake of being near her and for the times when they walked hand in hand in the dark along the Barbican ... all for the joy of a handful of chaste kisses and the delight of watching the changing moods across her face, her blue eyes radiant with gaiety or dark with displeasure — until the day came when the old fever to spread his wings and go had returned. On the spur of the moment he got a berth on a Norwegian timber ship and sailed away, swearing love for ever — she to wait and he to make his fortune — and regular letters posted from every port he touched. Write he had, but not from every port, until once a month became now and then, and finally — after she had married someone else — even a friendly yearly letter was often missed. But Jimmy, my boy, he mused, the thin thread of past bliss still holds. Old acquaintance should never be forgot entirely, and certainly not — in his present moment of adversity — a fine woman like Kathy, free now, and wealthy from the chain of restaurants her husband had built up and sold for a fortune.

He lit another cheroot and began to stroll back to his hotel. Plymouth had changed, but not the Barbican much. Parked cars jammed the quay where horses and carts had once moved, some of the old pubs survived and there was a new one called the Sir Francis Chichester, and there was a rash of antique and gift shops for tourists. But lying alongside were still the fishing boats, coloured and dirty, their names reading now in the same kind of litany which had stirred his blood as a boy ... *Twilight, Hopeful, Petit Michel, Seaspray, Lucky Lady* ... and everywhere the smell of ropes and oil.

He quickened his steps a little. Just time for him to have a freshen up and a quick drink before Kathy arrived for lunch. Or, maybe, two drinks. After all this time, with nothing between them but a handful of letters most of his pretty coloured, a man needed a little stimulant to get into his best form. And best form it had because the till was nearly empty.

Katherine Trent (now Preston) enjoyed the lunch with Jimmy. He had always been good company and a great one for ever-embroidering his tales. Although he had been her first love she had in the fullness of time realised that it had only been the shadow of the real love to come. She had been happy in her marriage and she was content with her present state — though that did not mean that she was hardened against any change in it.

Coffee and liqueurs between them, they sat now in the sun lounge, a distinguished, prosperous looking man and a good-looking woman who had taken care of h appearance and still did.

137

Smiling, Jimmy raised his glass and said "Well, here's to us and that day long ago when I knocked basket of whitings out of your hand."

Smiling, Kathy shook her head. "Your memory's bad, Jimmy. They were herrings."

"Herrings, whitings, what does it matter? The great thing is here we are together and you sitting there and just the sight of you makes my heart bump again as it did that first day on the Barbican."

"Don't tell me that no one else has made your bump since those days," she said, teasing, her blue eyes full of laughter.

"Bump it's gone now and then, but never in the way you made it. Not enough, anyway, to tempt me into marriage. But what matter? I've had a full life, a successful one, and I've seen the world."

"And now?"

"And now, Kathy, I can sit back, stop worshipping the goddess of success and … well, let's say … begin to make my prayers to the goddess of love."

Kathy shook her head. "Not you, Jimmy. You were born with restless feet. No woman could hold you."

"You think not? Well, maybe so. But it's a bold one who throws out a challenge to Cupid. An arrow at random and even someone like myself becomes a happy victim. Still, let Cupid do what Cupid will. Today is our day. The sun shines and out there —" he nodded through the window, "— the car waits to waft us back to the old places of town and country where sweet memory still lingers fragrantly in the air."

Standing outside the hotel was a gleaming Rolls-Royce with a uniformed chauffeur at the wheel.

"Yours?" For a moment Kathy wondered if she had made a mistake in her private assessment of Jimmy's financial state.

"No, hired. A chariot fit for a princess. Come!" He rose and held out a hand to her.

Although she had not expected anything like this and had other appointments that afternoon, Kathy went with him. There was only one Jimmy and no wish in her heart to deny him, and as she went out with him she wondered, calmly, what her life would have been like if all those years back she had married him. Full of ups and downs, tears and laughter and restless roving, no doubt. But maybe, just maybe, there was something which could have grown between them which would have made it all worth while.

They spent that afternoon driving along the coast and then over the moors.. They stopped at places which in the old days they had reached by bicycle, stood on a headland and looked down to a little cove where they had bathed in the golden days. Unbidden in Kathy — though she did not trust Jimmy an inch — there was now and then the sharp stir of emotion and also — more surprising — sudden outbursts of laughter as he teased and joked with her which made her realise that it had been long since she had felt so open to flattery and gallant attentions, or recalled so strongly the nostalgia of days when they had walked hand in hand along the dusk-shadowed Barbican to stand in some doorway to shelter their long goodnight kisses.

Lying in bed that night Jimmy, reviewing the day, felt he had made good progress. But progress, my boy, he told himself, is one thing. Planning is another. Movement without objective is idle vagrancy. Which should he opt for? An invitation to her to invest in one of his mythical companies ... say a couple of thousand to put him on his way again? Or go for the jackpot of marriage, snare her in the silken meshes of love ... and then with marriage to cushion the blow come clean about his affairs? Well, no need to decide yet. Time would set the right straw blowing in the breeze.

And Time, obligingly, did.

For a week Jimmy courted Kathy with lunches, dinners, flowers, the green chauffeur driven Rolls-Royce, and long trips through Devon and Cornwall in the fast burgeoning spring, until finally Kathy invited him to dinner at her house, giving him as a first course a dish of whiting with their tails curled into their mouths, and then a steak-and-kidney pudding which had been his favourite in the old days when he had eaten and worked at the restaurant. They sat together afterwards, Kathy wearing the orchid he had sent her, and Jimmy smoking a fine Havana cigar, while a glass of brandy stood at his side. It was the brandy on top of the wines at dinner which tipped the scales for Jimmy, freeing his already facile tongue and over-colouring the deep longing his mind for a safe and comfortable anchorage after years of adventuring with a fine woman like Kathy to share it.

He said, "The Rolls will be here for me in a few love. It's a feast for the gods you have given me. Nowhere in the world have I

139

ever eaten better — and why should it not be because the true hearth and the true joy is where the heart of a man settles like a bird to a warm nest. You were a golden haired princess when 1 first saw you, and you sit there now like a golden haired queen — and to both I have been and still am a slave —"

"Oh Jimmy — no slave you. A buccaneer, yes."

"Oh that I were a pirate to carry to happiness in some far El Dorado! But I say no more. You know what is in my heart. These past days have been a paradise. A paradise from which I would never stray as so foolishly I strayed all those years ago. I go no further into the exactitude of words or emotions. You know what is in my heart and you know what is in yours. Let it all rest there until tomorrow. If there is to be joy, a great calm joy for us bath, then I shall be waiting for you at lunch. But if you don't come ... Ah, well, then a man like myself knows that sometimes the gods give and sometimes they take and humble mortals must abide their will."

When he had gone Kathy sat by the dying fire for a long time. There had never been any doubt in her mind that Jimmy had come back to borrow money from her or interest some grand scheme which would show her a handsome profit — but that he would ask her to marry him had only slowly over the past days become apparent. He was a well set up man a woman could take pride in, but if he had five hundred pounds to bless his name with she would be surprised. It would be no surprise to her if the car hire firm and the hotel never saw their money ... She smiled and. shook her head with gentle despair over him. A. handful of happy days refreshing old memories and the past raptures of first love she had thoroughly enjoyed, but to take Jimmy as a husband would be folly, even though she was wealthy enough to indulge her follies. Jimmy and the boy on the Barbican were still the same... rainbow chasers, romantic dreamers. Compared with her husband, steady, unromantic, shrewd in business and no matter his true love for her never for once unpredictable or irrationally extravagant, Jimmy would be golden-edged trouble, a man who valued the joy of laughter and wild impulse more than any solid investment and security,

She stood up and said aloud firmly, "No, Jimmy, my sweetheart, even though I could afford you and there's still love of a kind in my heart for you, you've come too late ... though I'm tempted. Oh, dear heart, I really am tempted."

*   *   *

Jimmy sat alone in his first-class carriage on the train to London, reading his paper, his suitcases on the rack above him, the air heavy with smoke from his cheroot. Outside in the corridor a youth of about eighteen sat on a suitcase, staring out at the racing fields and hills. Eying him, Jimmy thought … second-class carriages all full. Well, youth must learn to travel steerage to begin with. Nice looking, well-set up boy — could have been me at that age. All the world before him. Aye, and maybe somewhere a girl he's promised to write to every week, and will — until time and chance change the pattern.

Looking at his watch, he got up, tucked his paper under his arm and went into the corridor. He gave the youth a smile and said, "Going to London?"

"Yes, sir."

"Sharp set?"

"Sir?"

"Like some lunch and a drink?"

"Well …"

"Come on then, I'll treat you. Come on, lad — on your feet. Never turn down a good offer. I never did when I was your age, and I never do now." He grinned. "We'll split a bottle of wine with our meal and you can tell me your brief life story. Follow me, laddie, to the rare delights of a British Rail meal." And then, to himself, added — and to the splitting of the last ten pound note my wallet.

At that same moment Kathy stood in the foyer of the hotel reading a note which Jimmy had left for her with the receptionist. Part of it read:

> *…I knew you would come, for like me your heart rules your head in the end. But there is a foolishness in me different from yours. A good berth and a fine woman with money and generosity to go with it I never thought to turn from, my dear heart — but I do because there's a decency even in foot-loose old Jimmy that forbids him — unexpectedly, I confess — to sully the purity of first*

141

love and these past few days with any taint of sordid self-interest ... though, my fair-haired princess of the Barbican I was sorely tempted. Farewell, my love. Addendum – they were whitings, not herrings.

Printed in Great
Britain
by Amazon